Anthony Davis

Acknowledgements

The author was in the studios or on location during the making of a number of the programmes recalled in this book, and interviewed some of the producers and stars at the time. Others have been interviewed at later dates. Some programmes, however, were seen only as a viewer at home, and two invaluable books consulted daily during the writing of this one are *Halliwell's Television Companion* (Paladin 1986) by Leslie Halliwell with Philip Purser, and the *Complete Encyclopedia of Television Programs 1947–1979* (Barnes/Yoseloff 1979) by Vincent Terrace.

The author and publishers gratefully acknowledge the following companies for use of pictures and thank them for their help:
ABC TV; ATC TV; BBC Enterprises Ltd (pp. 61, 69, 71); Central TV (p. 66); Columbia Pictures Industries Inc.; ITC Ltd; © Keystone Collection (p. 99); Lorimar Inc.; MCA TV Universal City Studios Inc.; Metromedia Producers Corporation; Metro Goldwyn Mayer TV; National Broadcasting Company., Inc; Screen Gems Inc.; International Film and TV Features (UPI); © Universal Pictorial Agency (p. 101); SKR Photos International.

First published in 1988 by Boxtree Limited.
Published in association with
Independent Television Books Ltd.

Text Copyright © Anthony Davis 1988

Designed by Groom and Pickerill
Typeset by Cambrian Typesetters, Frimley, Surrey
Printed in Italy
for Boxtree Limited, 36 Tavistock Street, London WC2E 7PB

British Library Cataloguing in Publication Data

Davis, Anthony, 1927–
    TV's greatest hits
    1. Television programmes – Critical
    studies
    I. Title
    791.45'75

ISBN 1–85283–237–1

Printed and bound in Italy by
IPE Amadeus s.p.a., Rome

Contents

Foreword

This book is about television series that have been enjoyed not just in the countries where they were made but around the world. Some have been seen in more than 100 countries, repeated many times and are still being shown. They are not necessarily among the best shows ever made, nor the most innovative – though some are both – but within their own categories they have been such hits that almost all viewers, everywhere, have heard their titles.

The book is not a history of television, though it traces many significant developments since the Fifties as it recalls hugely popular programmes sometimes ignored in academic works.

The selling of programmes is a competitive business, and no comprehensive, comparative sales charts exist. Even if they did, they would be unreliable guides to popularity because one deal to America can earn more than 40 to Third World countries, and while some programmes get peaktime networked screenings others are consigned to late-night slots or minority channels, or both. For example, consider the British presentation of two American police series: *Kojak* was shown throughout Britain at peak time on BBC1, but *Hill Street Blues* was first seen on different days and at different times in some, but not all, ITV regions. Even when it won a nationwide showing, this was on Channel 4, which has a minority share of the audience. And while some series are still being repeated and sold to new markets years after production ceased, the appeal of others has evaporated quickly.

So the programmes dealt with are based on lists obtained from production and distribution companies of their own best-sellers, interpreted with some circumspection. To keep the book within bounds, it is confined to programmes from America and Britain, and to series, which are more saleable than single programmes.

Inevitably, some readers will be disappointed that their favourite programmes are not mentioned, which in many cases may be because these programmes are not the big sellers they imagine. For instance, *Maigret*, though remembered fondly, does not rank with *Miss Marple* in BBC sales, and *Minder* is not – as yet, at any rate – as big a seller for Thames as *The Sweeney*. Even so, 200 series are recalled.

Introduction

In France it was *Chapeau Melon et Bottes de Cuir* (Bowler Hat and High Leather Boots). In West Germany it was *Mit Schirm, Charm und Melone* (With Umbrella, Charm and Bowler Hat). In England, where the series was made, and in the United States and other English-language countries, it was *The Avengers*. Subtitled or dubbed into foreign languages, television's biggest hits have been seen around the world.

In the Sixties, when the Western, *Bonanza*, was being shown in 60 countries and had a weekly viewing audience estimated at 400 million, its leading actor, Lorne Greene, joked: 'We are America's number two export – just ahead of Coca-Cola and right behind foreign aid.'

In recent years *The Boys from the Blackstuff* has been seen in Russia, *Yes Minister* in Dubai, *Some Mothers Do 'Ave Em* in Turkey, *Tenko* in Malaysia – and none of these yet ranks among the BBC's biggest sellers. *The Muppet Show* has been seen by 300 million in more than 100 countries and has been dubbed into seven languages.

Television has not always crossed frontiers. The international market in TV programmes began to develop only in 1955. Before then the number of countries with regular daily TV services was small, and most television was live. Videotape recording had yet to be invented, and telerecording – the system of transferring TV pictures to film – gave poor quality, so to repeat a programme it was usually performed again, as in the theatre.

Some programmes were, of course, made on film and therefore could be repeated, duplicated and offered for sale, but there was little co-operation from the film industry, which regarded TV, justifiably, as an unwelcome competitor for its cinemas, and felt that if it could be deprived of films it might not survive.

However, as TV aerials continued to sprout above rooftops, resistance began to crumble. In 1951 Lucille Ball began making *I Love Lucy* on film in a fringe Hollywood studio. A year later, filming of Jack Webb's *Dragnet* began, and in 1954 the Walt Disney organisation made a deal with America's ABC network to provide a *Disneyland* series on film.

Warner Brothers was the first of Hollywood's major studios to break ranks. It agreed to make 40 hour-long films for ABC Television which, with 12 repeats, would give the network a programme a week for a year in the 1955–56 season. Under the umbrella title, *Warner Brothers Presents*, there were three series in rotation: *Casablanca*, based on the 1942 film (but with Charles McGraw in the Humphrey Bogart role), *King's Row*, derived from a 1941 Ann Sheridan movie, and *Cheyenne*, inspired by a 1947 Western. *Cheyenne* was the show of which least was expected, but it was the biggest hit and soon became a series in its own right.

Other major studios followed Warner's lead. Fox, Columbia, Republic and MGM formed subsidiaries to make half-hour and one-hour TV programmes, many of them Westerns because of the success of *Cheyenne*, and by the end of 1957 more than 100 filmed series were in production.

When commercial TV opened in Britain in 1955 it provided a ready-made market for these series. There were no language problems and as the American producers had already recouped their costs in the US, they could offer the programmes cheaply, for what they earned was all profit. The British ITV companies, whose aim was to provide more popular entertainment than the BBC service, which some of them derided as 'auntyish', could acquire programmes of proven appeal more cheaply than making new ones.

So, in ITV's opening week in 1955 (when it was available only in London), Britons were introduced to the first American programmes they had ever seen; *I Love Lucy* and *Dragnet*. These were instantly popular; many viewers found the American filmed programmes slicker than anything they had been accustomed to from the BBC. But it was not a one-way traffic. With an eye on what was happening in the US, companies had begun filming programmes in Britain before ITV went on the air, and *The Adventures of Robin Hood*, filmed at Nettlefold studio, was shown on the CBS network in America within days of its opening in England on ITV.

By 1958 commercial television had been established in 26 countries and a new industry had grown up, subtitling or dubbing American programmes into foreign languages. A film was cut into short sequences which were spliced to make loops, and projected to actors who then recorded the translation. Dubbing was already being carried out in France, Italy, Japan, Hong Kong, Egypt, Lebanon, Mexico and Cuba.

In Britain Lew Grade (later Sir Lew, and now Lord Grade) was a pioneer of transatlantic programme selling, commissioning escapist series with a mid-Atlantic accent and at least one token American actor in the cast to help sales in the US. Not everyone approved, and the BBC and some ITV companies continued conscientiously to make programmes with only the home market in mind, offering them abroad almost as an afterthought. Consequently, it was longer before the BBC made an impact overseas, though eventually the potential rewards made the world market impossible to disregard.

The invention of videotape at the end of the Fifties was to make more programmes available for sale, though it took some years to come into general use, and for even more years buyers preferred the quality and pace obtained with film.

Since then rising costs have led to co-productions (in which TV organisations in different countries share the financing of expensive programmes) and pre-sale agreements (under which a programme is sold to television in another country before being made). Most big-budget British productions are now pre-sold, and thereby guaranteed wider viewing audiences.

The opening of new broadcast channels and cable networks, and the extension of broadcasting hours through the day and night, have meant an increased demand for programme material and new leases of life for old programmes. So viewers who were not born when *The Adventures of Robin Hood* and *Sergeant Bilko* were first screened are familiar with them through re-runs. *The Untouchables* (first seen in 1959), *The Flintstones* (1960) and *Dr Kildare* (1961) were all still to be seen on British television in 1988. Other veteran programmes are being made available on videocassettes. They all rank among television's biggest hits.

1
They Rode Thataway

The Westerns

The first worldwide television successes were Westerns, which, although uniquely American, could easily be understood by viewers of all ages and in all countries. They depended on action, and the spectacle of Indians pursuing a stage coach or outlaws robbing a bank needed no explanation. The spare dialogue involved no subtleties, commonly consisting of such terse lines as 'Go for your gun', or 'We'll head 'em off at the pass'. The plots were elemental, pitting good men against bad, the scenery could be attractive, and the world had always enjoyed Westerns in the cinema, whence came the first TV hits – intended primarily for children.

They were shortened versions of the *Hopalong Cassidy* movies that had been made for the cinema since 1935, starring William Boyd and his horse Topper, until in 1948 the prematurely white-haired Boyd, who had bought the television rights to the character, began co-producing and starring in 100 new *Cassidy* adventures for television.

Ironically, the original Cassidy of Clarence E. Mulford's stories was wizened, stunted, tobacco chewing, hard drinking and swearing, with a mean streak and a limp (hence the nickname Hopalong), but Boyd transformed him into a hero – without any impediment. When asked about the Hopalong name he explained that Cassidy acquired it when he limped as a result of a wound, which had since healed. Said Boyd: 'He embodies all that is desirable, reassuring and exciting in life. He is a good Samaritan,

a pal to children, and gets through to parents too. He is law, order, honour and bravery personified, a cowboy hero with a halo round his head.'

The series led to an early merchandising campaign involving hats, guns, shirts and spurs, and its Bar 20 Ranch was regarded as a second home by millions of children who joined 'Hoppy's Troopers', and promised to obey 'Hoppy's Code of Conduct', which emphasised the virtues of loyalty, honesty, kindliness and ambition. Boyd commented:

'This was no ordinary role. Children hang on Hoppy's every word and action. One of the most humbling experiences of my life occurred at a big parade in Toronto, Canada. I was in full cowboy dress, down to a pair of matching pistols, and the rain was beating down on the crowds and the procession. Suddenly I realised that all along the line children were squirming out of their raincoats and hiding them. Hoppy wasn't wearing one and they weren't going to let Hoppy see they were cissies. . . . Altogether Hopalong Cassidy adds up to an admirable, ageless character who is right for youngsters of any generation. There's no reason why he shouldn't ride the TV trail for ever.'

Boyd might have been right – except that the programmes, in black and white, became obsolescent when television acquired colour. Before that the black-hatted *Hopalong Cassidy* was followed by the white-hatted *The Lone Ranger* on his horse, Silver. Originally created for radio in 1933, and in the cinema from 1938, the character reached television in 1949, and more than 220 episodes over 16 years were followed by a series of animated cartoon adventures.

The hero was a Texas Ranger, John Reid, sole survivor of an ambush by the Butch Cavendish Hole in the Wall gang. He had been left for dead in a valley but found by Tonto, a Potawatomie Indian, while out hunting. Tonto owed him a debt because Reid had cared for Tonto as a child, when renegade Indians had killed his family, so Tonto nursed back to health the man he called 'kemo sabe' (meaning 'faithful friend'), and subsequently followed him everywhere. To conceal from the outlaws that one Ranger had remained alive to avenge his comrades, Reid adopted a black mask, and always vanished before he could be thanked by those he aided. On television the Lone Ranger was first played by Clayton Moore, later by John Hart; Tonto by Jay Silverheels, a Canadian-born Mohawk.

Programmes opened with a voice-over: 'A fiery horse with the speed of light, a cloud of dust and a hearty "Hi-yo Silver!" The Lone Ranger! With his faithful Indian companion, Tonto, the daring and resourceful masked rider of the plains led the fight for law and order in the early West. Return with us now to those thrilling days of yesteryear; the Lone Ranger rides again!'

The Cisco Kid, which followed books, films as early as 1929, comic strips and radio serials, is now mainly noteworthy as the first TV series to be filmed in colour. That was in 1951, when colour transmissions in the US were in an experimental stage, two years before the introduction of a system capable of being received equally well on both colour and black and white receivers, and 16 years before colour began in Europe.

Cowboy heroes had tended to wear conservative clothes, but the Cisco Kid affected gaudy shirts, silver spurs and a king-size sombrero. Amiable and flirtatious, he fought badmen in New Mexico, righting wrongs, protecting the weak and dispensing justice. 'Here's adventure. Here's romance. Here's O'Henry's famous Robin Hood of the Old West, the Cisco Kid,' ran the introductory announcement.

The Kid was played by Duncan Renaldo, who was born in New Jersey of Spanish descent, and educated in Madrid and Paris. He had played the character in movies since 1945. His horse was Diablo, and he was accompanied by a food-loving Mexican sidekick, Pancho (veteran actor Leo Carrillo), who provided comedy by mangling the English language with such pleas as: 'Ceesco, let's went!' Violence was minimal; the Kid never raised his gleaming .44 in anger, and Renaldo assured parents: 'I'm just as concerned about your children as I am about my own. I promise they'll see nothing on *The Cisco Kid* that I wouldn't want my own children to watch.'

Even more saintly were the singing cowboy stars of *The Gene Autry Show* and *The Roy Rogers Show*, whose rival series, in which they appeared under their own names, began at the start of the Fifties. They were as clean in their clothes as in their deeds, Autry's wardrobe including some 300 embroidered and sequinned outfits. Autry and his horse Champion were based on his Melody ranch, where he raised horses and walnuts. Rogers and his wife, Dale Evans, and their horses Trigger and Buttercup, lived on the Double R.

Lawmen

These and other Westerns were seen in Britain on ITV, and also in France, Italy, Japan and South America, the voices dubbed into the local languages by local actors, and were followed by so-called adult Westerns, made for peak time, rather than early evening slots. The first, in 1955, was *The Life and Legend of Wyatt Earp*, starring Hugh O'Brian. It was about the lawman with the sweeping moustache who lived from 1848 to 1929, and was in turn marshal of Dodge City, Kansas, and Tombstone, Arizona, armed with a Buntline Special, a .45 calibre six-gun which could be fitted with a shoulder piece for long-range shooting. The studio props department provided 500 blanks a week for the series which ran to 266 episodes over six years.

Historians of the old West have different views about Earp. O'Brian's was: 'He's a controversial character who has been depicted as everything from saint to devil, lawman to bully, loquacious to taciturn. So I

First of the TV cowboys, William Boyd as Hopalong Cassidy in the 1940s.

devoted seven months to reading about Earp, and I'm convinced that he was a thoroughly honest man, righteous and utterly fearless. He was also just. Wyatt was a fantastic individual. He had tremendous courage and, what was unusual among so many of his ilk, he was highly intelligent. Wyatt had 140 gunfights and was never wounded. He never had a scratch on him from a gun battle to the day he died. This in itself is obviously an incredible thing, considering the dangerous life he led. He always preferred to avoid violence and, unlike so many others of his day, frowned on killing except where it was absolutely necessary.

15

James Arness spent 20 years in the role of Marshal Matt Dillon in Gunsmoke.

Wyatt tried to rap his adversary over the head with his long-barrelled gun, or tried to out-think him.'

Wyatt Earp was a half-hour series, and so was *Gunsmoke*, which began in the US a few days later, but this was to be a phenomenal success and moved to hour-long episodes in colour in 1961. It came from radio, where it had begun three years earlier, starring William Conrad (later television's *Cannon*), and was to be the most enduring of all Westerns – in production for 20 years. It moved away from the stereotype Western stories, dealt with real issues, and had rounded human characters. The hero, Matt Dillon, marshal of Dodge City, stoical and somewhat humourless, was played by 6 ft 6 in-tall James Arness, a reclusive man

of Norwegian descent who had been wounded at Anzio in World War Two. Hitherto a small-part actor, he was a protégé of the greatest of Western movie stars, John Wayne, who put him under contract and when offered the part of Dillon, suggested Arness.

Dillon, whose horse was confusingly named Marshal, thought as well as fought, assisted by a lame deputy, Chester Goode (Dennis Weaver) until 1963; and afterwards by hillbilly Festus Haggen (Ken Curtis). Other regulars were crusty Dr Galen Adams, generally known as 'Doc' (Milburn Stone), who dug bullets out of Dillon, and Kitty Russell (Amanda Blake) of the Longbranch saloon. In 244 episodes, according to a statistician, the hardboiled Kitty got through 900 shots of whisky and 365 glasses of beer, and smashed 27 bottles over the heads of objectionable customers. Originally she

Little Joe Cartwright (Michael Landon) in a tough spot in Bonanza; *one of the many over 13 years.*

Steve McGarrett (Jack Lord) wears the only blue suit on the island in Hawaii Five-O.

It's a cover up. The snappy hat hides the bald dome of Telly Savalas in Kojak.

Below left *David Soul and Paul Michael Glaser, heartthrob heroes of Starsky and Hutch.*

Below right *Sharon Gless and Tyne Daly, the policewoman buddies of Cagney and Lacey.*

appeared to be anybody's, but after women viewers complained about her apparent easy availability, the studio gave her more modest dresses and made her the saloon's owner with an implied allegiance to Dillon, though they never married. Arness said:

'People like Westerns because they represent a time of freedom. A cowboy wasn't tied down to one place or one woman. When he got mad he hauled off and slugged someone. When he drank, he got good and drunk. Today people don't have enough gumption to live the way they want to. They've grown away from their basic instincts. They're over-civilised. That is why they tune in to Western shows, to escape from conformity. And they certainly don't want to see a US marshal come home and help his wife with the dishes.'

The 20 years that Arness spent playing Dillon were thought to be longer than any real marshal of Dodge City survived, and the series was still among America's top 30 shows when production ended in 1975.

Wanderers

Cheyenne was an hour-long series (though in black and white) from the start, and had another laconic hero. Cheyenne Bodie was played by Clint Walker, another 6 ft 6 in giant, who as Norman Walker had been

Clint Walker seizes an opportunity to bare his giant torso in Cheyenne.

successively a seaman, sheet metal worker, carpenter, vacuum cleaner salesman, insurance agent, truck driver, construction worker, prospector, cattle puncher on a Texas ranch, night club bouncer and private detective. Then he met actor Van Johnson who introduced him to an agent. His first role of any substance was that of Bodie.

Bodie was a rootless enigma. There was no Kitty in his life. He lent his arm to anyone who needed it, and took a lot of beatings as a result. Walker had a theory that the audience enjoyed seeing big men take punishment – even when they were heroes. But in 1958 he quarrelled with Warners about the terms and restrictions of his contract, as a result of which he was suspended, and to show him his place, Warners brought in a new leading character, Bronco Layne, a wandering ex-Confederate army captain, played by 6 ft 2 in Ty Hardin. However, the show's popularity suffered, and Walker was recalled in 1959, while Hardin continued to play Layne in a series called *Bronco*.

Have Gun, Will Travel in 1957 starred craggy-faced Richard Boone, who had once understudied Sir John Gielgud in the Greek tragedy *Medea* on the New York stage. Boone played the uncommunicative, mysterious Paladin. The word means a knightly hero, and Paladin's trademark, which decorated his black leather holster, was a white chess knight. In the holster was a Colt .45 single action gun with a 7½-inch barrel. Paladin was an educated ex-army officer, a wealthy man-about-town in San Francisco where he lived in the Carlton Hotel, with servants Hey Boy and Hey Girl (Kam Tong and Lisa Lu), and a hired gun in the country. His business cards read: 'Have Gun – Will Travel. Wire Paladin, San Francisco.'

Humour was not a strong point of early Westerns – beyond a comic cook or deputy, until *Maverick*, a tongue-in-cheek Western starring James Garner and Jack Kelly in 1957. Garner explained the title in these words: 'A maverick is a drifter, a tramp, and the word comes from an old Texas rancher, Samuel Maverick, who didn't brand his cattle. Thus a wandering animal with no particular brand became a maverick.'

Garner played Bret Maverick, a fast-talking gambler, roving the West with decks of cards, and relying on guile rather than guns to extricate himself from trouble with losing players and law men. Garner said at the time:

'He's a strange sort of hero. More of an anti-hero. He's a gambling man interested much more in himself than in ideals or justice. Not much of a gunman either. He likes the good life and the girls and, as far as he's concerned, the poor can fight their own battles.'

The idea behind *Maverick*, according to producer Roy Huggins, was to turn conventional Westerns like *Cheyenne* inside out. 'I wanted to see how many rules we could break and get away with it,' he said.

Brother Bart, played by Kelly, was introduced when production schedules brought time problems. One crew shot his scenes, the other Garner's. Then, when Garner left, after sueing Warners for breach of contract, Roger Moore – not yet a movie star – replaced him as Beau Maverick, an English cousin.

The original series ran four years and in 1981, after *The Rockford Files*, Garner returned in a revival, though he declared at the outset: 'I'm 20 years older now, and so is Maverick. I'm not going to be on the screen for one solid hour and I'm not going to get the hell kicked out of me any more.'

Long Treks

Wagon Train, which also began in 1957, was the story of a pilgrimage westward from Missouri to California. Ward Bond played Major Seth Adams, the leader, and Robert Horton supported him as Flint McCullough, a young scout. A big budget series, it was based on the 1950 John Ford film *Wagonmaster*, in which Bond, a Hollywood veteran of more than 200 Western movies, also appeared. Its strength was that different characters were encountered every week, joining or leaving the trek, and they were played by guest stars. Among them: Ricardo Montalban, Ernest Borgnine, Agnes Moorehead, Sterling Hayden, Shelley Winters, Dan Duryea, George Montgomery, Lee Van Cleef, Linda Darnell, John Carradine, Lou Costello, Cliff Robertson, Charles Bickford, William Bendix, James Coburn, Jane Wyman, Virginia Mayo, Rhonda Fleming,

Dorothy Provine, Anne Baxter, Ann Blyth, John Wayne, Ronald Reagan, Joan Blondell, Burgess Meredith, Bette Davis and Mickey Rooney.

Bond was 57 when he died on location in 1960 after a heart attack; the strenuous role is thought to have hastened his death. But *Wagon Train* rolled on, with John McIntire, a Montana cattle rancher as well as an actor,

Humour comes to the West in Maverick; *Jack Kelly, Roger Moore and Robert Colbert.*

replacing Bond as new trail boss, Chris Hale. Horton, who had quit (later to star in *A Man Called Shenandoah* as a cowboy trying to discover his identity after being found on the prairie wounded and suffering amnesia), was replaced by Robert Fuller

A young Clint Eastwood, with Paul Brinegar as Wishbone, the cook, in Rawhide.

(formerly of *Laramie*). In 1963 the programmes were expanded from a nominal hour to 75 minutes, and the series was shown in colour, but the wagon train was nearing the end of the trail. After another 32 episodes it ended in 1965.

However, in 1959 there were more than 30 Westerns in every week's schedules on American TV, and five of the Top 10 programmes were Westerns. One of them was *Rawhide*, the continuing story of a cattle drive from San Antonio, Texas, to Sedalia, Kansas. The title song, with its whipcracking refrain of 'Move 'em on, head 'em up . . . Rawhide', was a big hit for singer Frankie Laine.

The programmes opened with a voice over a scene of the cattle drive: 'This is the landscape of Rawhide: desert, forest, mountain and plains. It is intense heat, bitter cold, torrential rain, blinding dust, men risking their lives, earning small reward – a life of challenge – Rawhide. It is men like trail scout Pete Nolan, the cantankerous Wishbone, Ramrod Rowdy Yates, good-natured Mushy, and trail boss Gil Favor. These men are Rawhide.'

Nolan was played by Sheb Woolley; Wishbone, the cook, by Paul Brinegar, and Mushy, the drover, by James Murdock. Eric Fleming starred as Gil Favor, and his right hand man, Rowdy Yates, was played by Clint Eastwood. A newspaper story in 1959 described Eastwood as 'one time athletics instructor and lumberjack . . . now turned, as he says, "actor, full-time – I hope." ' It was his impact in *Rawhide* that caused an Italian company to invite him to make a film in Spain, and so begin the series of spaghetti Westerns that made him a superstar.

Family Affairs

Bonanza, which also began in 1959, started a new trend in Westerns – the family saga, akin to soap opera. It purported to be set on the Ponderosa Ranch, on the outskirts of Virginia City, Nevada, during the Civil War, soon after the discovery of the Comstock silver lode, though, in fact, the Ponderosa did not exist. The shows were made in a studio.

Canadian actor Lorne Greene starred as Ben Cartwright, a patriarchal widower running a vast ranch of 1,000 square miles of timbered land with the aid of three sons born to him by different wives. The oldest was Adam (Pernell Roberts), thoughtful and balanced; his brothers were Eric, always known as Hoss (Dan Blocker), a gentle giant, 6 ft 4 in tall and weighing more than 21 stone, and Little Joe (Michael Landon), young and hot-headed. Essentially it was about the bonds between four strong men who lived for each other, protecting their land, fighting corruption, and helping others.

Greene was less than happy with the early programmes. He said of Ben Cartwright later: 'He loved his timberlands – fanatically. He loved his sons – fanatically. He pounded the Bible – fanatically. And he said things like, "Fire and brimstone." He was a bore. After the first two episodes I wanted to throw in my hand.' However, after studio conferences the character became more human.

In Britain, where *Bonanza* began in 1960, it was one of the key programmes, along with home-grown shows such as *Sunday Night at the London Palladium*, that helped establish ITV, then expanding across the country, to become the most popular channel. British homes were named 'Ponderosa' after the Cartwright ranch, and when the Queen met Lorne Greene in Canada in 1964 she told him that she and her children watched the show regularly on ITV.

By 1965 the series was so entrenched that it could survive the departure of the oldest son, when Pernell Roberts, who played Adam, had him written out in order to return to the stage. *Bonanza* made dollar millionaires of the regular trio that remained – Greene, Blocker and Landon. The £7,500 per episode they reputedly received was dwarfed by the fees for repeat showings, and the income from appearances at rodeos, conventions, and in other TV programmes. But in May 1972, two weeks before the start of shooting on a new series, Blocker, the massive and much-loved Texan, was rushed into hospital where he died of thrombosis.

His colleagues expected the show to end then, but it went on, even beyond September when Greene collapsed with what was diagnosed as a mild heart attack; in November, however, the network decided to close the Ponderosa, after more than 400 hours of the programme. Michael Landon gave the news to the studio technicians and wept. 'It is the passing of an era,' he mourned. The crew donned black armbands as the men of the Ponderosa rode out for the last time.

Bonanza influenced two other family Westerns, *The Big Valley* and *The High Chaparral*. The first, which began in 1965, shortly before *Bonanza* ended, was the story of a cattle-ranching family in the San Joaquin Valley of California, and featured a matriarch. Victoria Barkley, a strong-willed widow, was played by silver-haired Hollywood veteran Barbara Stanwyck, and her family comprised Jarrod (Richard Long), her eldest son, a lawyer; Nick (Peter Breck), her hot-headed second son who acted as ranch foreman; Eugene (Charles Briles), her shy youngest son; Audra (Linda Evans), her impulsive daughter; and Heath (Lee Majors), her late husband's illegitimate son born of an Indian girl.

The High Chaparral, which came two years later, concerned the Cannon family: Big John (Leif Erickson), his wife Victoria (Linda Cristal), his brother Buck (Cameron Mitchell), and his none-too-bright son, Blue (Mark Slade), on a Tucson, Arizona, ranch in the 1870s beset by drought, Cochise and 600 restless Indians, and a Mexican cattle baron wanting the land.

The West in Decline

The Virginian (1962) was television's first 90-minute, or movie-length, series. Its theme was the destruction of the Western way of life by progress from the East. Based on a novel by Owen Wister, it was set on the Shiloh Ranch in Medicine Bow, Wyoming, owned by Judge Henry Garth (Lee J. Cobb), in the 1880s. The Virginian of the title was the stern, silent foreman of the ranch (James Drury), a mysterious drifter whom everyone respected but no one really knew. Doug McClure played Trampas, his wild assistant.

In 1970 the series became *The Men from Shiloh*, moved on in time to 1890, and Lee Majors and Stuart Whitman joined the cast. The ranch was now owned by Col. Alan MacKenzie, an Englishman (Stewart Granger), which caused surprise to some viewers, though Granger declared: 'It amazes me that people were surprised that an Englishman should be cast as a Western rancher. Many of the big ranching spreads in the West were run by Englishmen.' For his own part, he reminded journalists: 'I've owned two

The High Chaparral; *John Cannon (Leif Erickson), his wife (Linda Cristal) and brother (Cameron Mitchell).*

The horseless carriage replaces the horse in Alias Smith and Jones, *one of the last Westerns.*

spreads, one in Arizona and one in New Mexico. I raised a magnificent strain of snow-white French beef cattle. I'm not a dude you know. I can ride and cowboy a bit.' But demand for those skills was soon to run out.

Alias Smith and Jones was, in 1971, the last hit Western, created to cash in on the success in cinemas of *Butch Cassidy and the Sundance Kid* with Paul Newman and Robert Redford. A Newman lookalike, Ben Murphy, played Jed 'Kid' Curry, and Pete Duel played Hannibal Heyes, bank robbers trying to go straight – largely because they had found the latest safes impossible to open. The governor of Kansas granted them a provisional amnesty, to become a complete pardon if they managed to lead blameless lives for a year, but in the meantime the decision was to remain a secret between the outlaws, the governor and Sheriff Lom Trevors (James Drury). So they left the Devil Hole gang and adopted aliases, Heyes calling himself Joshua Smith, and Curry taking the name Thaddeus Jones.

Duel, who had a drink problem, committed suicide in December 1971 by putting a bullet through his head beneath the Christmas tree in his home. Roger Davis, a friend, formerly the narrator of the series, replaced him for another year. But the Western boom was over. The sound of six-guns, which had echoed around the world, was becoming sporadic. *Gunsmoke* was the only Western on the screen in America by the time its production was ended in 1975, and Westerns on television have since consisted of re-runs of old series, or movies. Several reasons have been advanced: concern about the level of violence and gunplay on the screen, the increased sophistication of viewers, making the simple stories of the Westerns out of tune with the times, and the advent of new genres such as secret agentry.

The simplest explanation is that the Westerns died of natural causes. As an American TV executive has said: 'People got fed up. The Western lasted for years and years and in the end the hackneyed old themes were totally exhausted. Viewers had enough and they wanted something different, I think the days of the US marshal riding in to clean up the town are probably gone for good.'

2
Here Come the Cops

Police Series

One type of television series which has never gone out of favour is the police drama, but there have been changes in style over the years. *Dragnet*, which began in 1951, showed police procedure in an almost documentary manner. The series, which Jack Webb devised, wrote, produced, and starred in as Sgt. Joe Friday, was based on cases of the Los Angeles Police Department and detailed the minutiae of investigation in an understated rather than over-dramatised way. Webb allowed no more than one bullet to be fired in every four episodes, and delivered lines, poker-faced, in an emotionless, laconic manner. The most famous lines were: 'My name's Friday, I'm a cop', and 'Just trying to get at the facts, ma'am'.

Each episode began with the announcement: 'Ladies and gentlemen, the story you are about to see is true. Only the names have been changed to protect the innocent.' Then Webb, as Joe Friday, declared: 'This is the city, Los Angeles, California. I work here. I carry a badge.'

The idea had come to Webb when he was playing a police lieutenant in a movie and his subsequent research was painstaking. Almost every night for two years he rode in police cars in San Francisco and Los Angeles. He was with police when they dealt with teenage gangs, warehouse thieves, safe-breakers, drunks and wife beaters. All the

time he studied how they handled people and how the public reacted. Every incident was filed in his mind for use in *Dragnet*, first on radio and then on television.

The police authorities liked the series and a reprint of some of Joe Friday's observations in it was issued to all officers in the LA force. It included Friday's advice to a rookie cop:

'You give up the normal life. Throw a party and that badge gets in the way. All of a

Fact-seeking in Dragnet*; Jack Webb as Sgt. Joe Friday (right) and Harry Morgan as Officer Gannon.*

Brod Crawford as Dan Matthews (left) confers with police motorcyclists in Highway Patrol.

sudden there isn't a straight man in the crowd. Everybody's a comedian. "Don't drink too much," somebody says, "or the man with the badge will run you in." Or "How's it goin', Dick Tracy? How many jay-walkers did you pinch today?" You'll fill out a report when you're right, you'll fill out a report when you're wrong; you'll fill out a report when you're not sure. You'll fill out one listing your leads, you'll fill out one when you have no leads. You'll make out a report on the reports you've made. You'll write enough words in your lifetime to stock a library. . . . There are over 5,000 men in this city who know that being a policeman is an endless, glamourless, thankless job that must be done. I know it too. And I'm damned glad to be one of them.'

Dragnet, which was the first American drama series ever seen on British television, when it began on ITV in 1955, ran to 300 episodes over seven years, by which time Friday was a lieutenant. It returned for another 100 in colour in 1967 with Friday, curiously, a sergeant again, partnered by Officer Bill Gannon (Harry Morgan, who later played Col. Sherman Potter in *M*A*S*H*).

Highway Patrol, which began in 1956, with burly, growling-voiced, broken-nosed Broderick Crawford as Dan Matthews, fast-talking chief of California's mobile force, also achieved some measure of authenticity, particularly by its use of radio call signs and number-coded messages exchanged between headquarters and the crews of patrol cars. 'Ten-four', meaning 'Message received and understood', and 'Ten-twenty', meaning 'Report your position', became catchphrases around the world, including Italy, where the series was known as *Policia della Strada*, and Spain where it was *Patrulla de Seguridad Carrera*.

The programme's opening announcement proclaimed: 'Whenever the laws of any state are broken, a duly authorised organisation swings into action. It may be called the State Police, State Troopers, Militia, the Rangers or the Highway Patrol. These are the stories of the men whose training, skill and courage have enforced and preserved our state laws.'

M Squad came into being in 1957 to do for Chicago what *Dragnet* had done for Los

Angeles, but the Chicago police, who had co-operated in a 1953 movie, and later regretted it, were less helpful. Despite this, 117 episodes were made. Co-producer and star was Lee Marvin, as Lt. Frank Ballinger, head of a special squad of plainclothesmen. (The M in the title was not explained; most viewers thought it stood for Murder.)

Marvin gave a remarkably cynical interview to the *New York Herald-Tribune* at the time:

'*Mr Marvin, why are you starring in, and producing, a crime show?*'

'Cops and robbers series sell. You don't make TV shows for fun, you make 'em for money.'

'*What makes your series different from the others now on TV?*'

'Me. We have the same script as all the others; the difference is in the acting and the direction.'

'*Are the Chicago police enthusiastic and co-operative about the series?*'

'Yeah, they arrested our cameramen twice. They go on the theory that there is no crime in Chicago.'

Lee Marvin as Lt. Frank Ballinger of the Chicago police in M Squad.

'*Is* M Squad *based on actual case histories?*'

'Of course not. We don't want realism. Fact disturbs an audience. We just want to entertain.'

'*Does* M Squad *have any special purpose or message?*'

'The purpose is to enable me to get rich so I can quit the show in three years. Then I'll go to Tahiti, take it real easy, and do the Gauguin bit with the paints.'

Inevitably, New York had then to be the setting for a series, and *Naked City*, which began in 1958, was filmed in its streets, each programme telling 'one of the eight million stories in the Naked City', according to the opening announcement. Unusual use was made of long shots, making the city the star rather than the actors, and passers by were seen as extras. To avoid confusion between real police and actors, the TV prowl cars were painted maroon and yellow instead of the police department's black and green; they looked authentic on black and white television.

The series was based on a 1948 movie of the same title, and the chief characters were originally Lt. Dan Muldoon (John McIntire) and Det. Jim Halloran (James Franciscus), but they were replaced by Lt. Mike Parker (Horace McMahon), Sgt. Frank Arcaro (Harry Bellaver) and Det. Adam Flint (Paul Burke) from 1960, after McIntire had moved on to *Wagon Train*.

Naked City made a feature of bizarre titles. A few of them were:

The Day the Island Almost Sank
The Corpse Ran Down Mulberry Street
Oftus Goofus
Today the Man Who Kills Ants Is Coming
The One Marked Hot Gives Cold
The King of Venus Will Take Care of You
Make It Fifty Dollars and Add Love to Nona
A Horse Has a Big Head, Let Him Worry
King Stanislaus and the Knights of the Round Stable
Robin Hood and Clarence Darrow, They Went Out with Bow and Arrow
Howard Running Bear Is a Turtle
No Naked Ladies in Front of Giovanni's House
$C_3H_5(NO_3)_3$

The Weekly Bloodbath

Crime series had been becoming more violent, driven by a ratings war between America's networks. A monitoring group in Los Angeles reported in 1960 that in one week TV showed 144 murders, 143 attempted murders, four attempted lynchings, two massacres or mass murders, 52 other killings, and 11 planned murders. The most criticised series, which had begun a year earlier, was *The Untouchables*, the story of federal agent Eliot Ness, leading a US Treasury Department team against bootlegging gangsters in Chicago during the Prohibition era of the Thirties. The agents were known as the Untouchables, because they could not be bought.

The real Ness had died in 1957, just after work started on the series; he had been looking forward to seeing himself portrayed on television, according to a friend. Ness was played by Robert Stack, the studio's third choice after Van Heflin and Van Johnson were unavailable.

With an eye on competing series, Quinn Martin, producer of *The Untouchables*, told his writers early on: 'More action – or we are going to get clobbered.' They obliged. Guns blazed as men in fedoras and double-breasted suits shot their way into speakeasies. Bodies littered the streets. *The Untouchables* was called 'the most violent show on television' and 'the weekly bloodbath'. Italian-Americans complained that the concentration on such thugs as the Neapolitan 'Scarface' Al Capone (played by Neville Brand) exposed them to odium.

During a public inquiry into TV violence in 1961 a startling exhibit was a letter from Quinn Martin to a writer which said: 'I wish you would come up with a different device than running the man down with a car, as we have done this now in three different shows.' *TV Guide* observed: 'In practically every episode a gangleader winds up stitched to a brick wall and full of bullets, or face down in a parking lot (and full of bullets), or hung up in an icebox, or run down in the street by a mug at the wheel of a big, black Hudson touring car.'

Production ended in 1963 after 114 episodes, though organised crime figured again in 1965 after television finally won permission from J. Edgar Hoover, the long-serving Director of the Federal Bureau of Investigation, to make a series based on FBI cases. Efrem Zimbalist Jr starred as Inspector Lew Erskine, a veteran of 30 years with the Bureau, who had helped hunt bank robbers John Dillinger and 'Baby Face' Nelson in the Thirties. In the story his wife had been killed in a gun battle, and his daughter Barbara (Lynn Loring) was in love with his fellow agent, Jim Rhodes (Stephen Brooks).

Zimbalist spent several weeks at the FBI academy seeing G-men trained in marksmanship, unarmed combat and interrogation techniques. The go-ahead for the series, however, was given only after the zealous and authoritarian Hoover had the results of a vetting of all the cast and crew. FBI agents checked on any convictions they might have had, their income tax returns and their drinking and gambling habits. Zimbalist found his fingerprints were already among the 173 millions in the FBI files; they had been taken, like those of all US servicemen, when he served in the forces in World War Two.

Hoover was pleased with *The FBI*, which, apart from showing G-men battling with gangsters, recognised the work of the Bureau's scientists in the laboratories established by Hoover. 'I have received hundreds of letters from people saying that the series portrayed what they thought FBI agents should be like,' he said. 'I want our own agents to live up to that image.' The series ran to more than 200 episodes over nine years.

Improbable Cops

Many viewers, however, had turned against realism and violence on the screen. As *The Untouchables* ended in 1963, a new style was being set by *Burke's Law*, in which Amos Burke, multi-millionaire captain of the Los Angeles homicide squad, dealt with crime from the comfortably upholstered rear seat of a Rolls-Royce. Producer Aaron Spelling told journalists at the time:

'This ain't gonna be no Mickey Spillane drama. There'll be no hoods in it; the criminals will be the kind who prey on high society in the grand manner. You won't be seeing violence either. We're doing something that's always been done in the cinema – shooting for glamour and forgetting about being too believable. The series will bring a tongue-in-cheek approach to the whole business. If you remember the *Thin Man* films and add the *Maverick* treatment, dripping with frothy satire, you have the format for *Burke*. Television is long overdue for the glamour treatment. We think that even a murder story can be humorous and well groomed.'

Dick Powell originally planned to play Burke but was unwell. He suggested David Niven, who was busy, and the choice fell upon Gene Barry who, Spelling said, 'looks like a playboy and acts like a millionaire'. All the episodes had titles beginning with the words, *Who Killed...?* and all featured famous guest stars – sometimes as many as ten in one programme. Spelling explained:

'There wasn't enough money in our safe to pay the sort of salaries these people normally command, so I gave them something else instead – a chance to play the sort of parts they've always wanted to play but never been given the chance. For example, Frankie Laine playing a guy who can't sing, and Juliet Prowse as a dancer with two left feet. Only the other day David Niven dropped by the studio and found himself with the part of a juggler.'

After two successful years the series was retitled *Amos Burke, Secret Agent* with Burke out of the police and in the world of espionage; the idea was to exploit the popularity of James Bond, but this was a mistake.

If a Rolls-riding policeman was improbable, a wheelchair-bound one was hardly less so, but in *Ironside* (from 1967) Raymond Burr, formerly television's Perry Mason, played Robert T. Ironside, San Francisco's chief of detectives, paralysed after being shot, but remaining a special consultant to the Police Department and heading a special team. The reason was explained by Burr:

'What happened was that we never thought that *Ironside* would make a series. We just did a two-hour movie in which Ironside was shot in the spine and the back and became paralysed. When it was so successful that they wanted to make a series out of the character there was no way we

Raymond Burr as crippled police chief in a wheelchair in Ironside.

could go back on that. But it turned out a plus. It gave a whole new edge to the character.'

Ironside was supposed to weigh 215 lb; Burr sometimes weighed considerably more. Many people were surprised to discover that away from the studio he was not himself confined to a wheelchair, for the Ironside image attached itself to the actor. One viewer gushed on meeting him: 'Oh, Mr Burr, I'm so happy you can walk now.' To which Burr responded simply: 'I'm happy too.'

Burr was philosophical about having to act in a seated position: 'I don't find working in a wheelchair confining. As an actor I find it challenging. An actor in a wheelchair has to learn to do many things sitting down that he would have done on his feet ordinarily. This changes the rhythm of the performance, the timing, the muscular control.'

Was it his scruffiness? Lt. Columbo (Peter Falk) has his credentials checked by a cop.

Not surprisingly, playing the part over eight years and through 180 episodes heightened his sympathy for the disabled: 'There are many people, incapacitated in many ways, not just paraplegics, who are being ignored,' he said. 'We kind of push them away into the dark. America is a bit more civilised than countries which don't allow their cripples in public sight, but not much.'

Hawaii Five-O had a more conventional hero in Steve McGarrett, a detective in a special branch of the Hawaiian police based in Honolulu, but essentially it was an escapist series. Though knifed bodies were found under waving palm trees and floating on the sea, the exotic locations discounted impressions of violence.

Jack Lord produced and starred, making more than 220 episodes over 11 years from

1968. As McGarrett he wore the only blue business suit on the island – an old and shiny one which concealed a shoulder holster. 'Book 'em, Danno,' McGarrett would crisply direct his partner, Det. Danny Williams (James MacArthur) after they captured villains. Rank and file police were played, not by actors or extras, but by off-duty Honolulu police who donated the money they earned to a police charity. The scenes of Hawaii provided a splendid background for films and television, as Lord said at the time. There were some drawbacks, however:

'When we first came to Hawaii there was nothing here – no studio, no trained personnel, no wardrobe department, nothing. Everybody said I was mad. Everything we needed had to be bought or flown in. The studio where we shoot interiors is a converted warehouse with no soundproofing. Often the rain on the roof, the nearby rifle range or simply passing trucks and planes, will hold up shooting, and the cost of living here is very high. Sometimes the winter rainy season brings storms that last for a week, but Hawaii is a Shangri-la for me, and I intend to live here for the rest of my life.'

He has, in fact, remained, his share of the profits multiplied by investment in American shopping centres.

Personality Cops

Given the unflagging popularity of crime series, the hunt for new detective characters is never-ending. Several were introduced under the umbrella title, *Mystery Movie*, at the start of the Seventies, the most successful being *Columbo*. Played by Peter Falk, he had first been seen in a TV movie four years earlier, after which everybody wanted to go on to make a weekly series; everybody, that is, except Falk. Eventually he agreed to make a mini-series of six episodes a year.

Lt. Columbo – his first name was never used – was scruffy, a Los Angeles homicide detective of unprepossessing appearance. Although rain is infrequent in California, he seldom shed a grubby, flapping raincoat. When he did, his suit was seen to be rumpled. His car looked even more ill-used. He chomped on the stub of a foul cigar, seemed perpetually short of money and did not own a credit card. In one episode, when he told a garage mechanic he was from the police department, the man asked, 'You under cover or sumpn?' People underestimated him, only to realise, to their regret, that behind the fumbling facade which irritated those he questioned was a tenacious investigator. Columbo was constantly on the prowl, working alone to ferret out inconsistencies in statements.

Whilst most TV investigators discuss their suspicions with subordinates or aides (a device to let viewers in on their thought processes) Columbo's technique was to confide his suspicions to the suspects. This apparent ineptitude led them to make mistakes. Falk said: 'He looks like a slob and most of the time he acts like one, but while he appears to be absorbing nothing he's actually absorbing everything.'

The killers in his world were highly paid executives and members of the jet set living in showplaces with pools and servants, but he was not intimidated. He remained amiable and unperturbed, asking his seemingly innocuous and irrelevant questions. Producer Everett Chambers claimed:

'We all can identify with Columbo, the little man, who proves that those who dwell in marble halls and dress in satin, often don't deserve it. In the end, they are done in by a man of street wit, who is afraid to fly, can't stand the sight of blood and never uses force.'

Columbo was particularly popular in Bulgaria, where episodes were first shown on Saturdays and repeated next day. Falk discovered this after a Bulgarian TV executive called the American ambassador for help with a problem; they had played every episode made, but were afraid that if they stopped showing the series it might be thought that the Communist authorities were clamping down on programmes from the West. Falk's help was sought, and given. He says: 'They took me – in that crumpled raincoat, of course – into a studio, and I had cue cards in phonetic Bulgarian that read: "It's all right. You're going to get more *Columbos* as soon as we make them. Don't blame your leaders or your government".'

Falk was reckoned to be the highest paid actor on television in 1977, when he was reputed to receive £320,000 per 90-minute episode – and still declined to make a weekly series. When negotiations over further episodes broke down, *Columbo* was replaced by *Kate Columbo*, starring Kate Mulgrew as the detective's resourceful wife. She had often been mentioned by him – 'Mrs Columbo is an amazing woman with many interests,' he would say – but never before seen. She was shown to be a self-sufficient superwoman with a part-time job on a newspaper in LA, who could take their car for repairs, drive their basset to the vet, attend a French lesson and solve a double murder in the course of a day, but she did not solve the studio's problem; Falk was not brought to heel.

Kojak, seen from 1973, was a complete contrast to *Columbo*. He was also a detective lieutenant, though in New York City, but he was sharper in appearance – affecting fancy waistcoats – and in manner, being abrasively outspoken with both his bosses and crooks, for whom he had a deep loathing, though he could be gentle with the oppressed. However, the most obvious peculiarities of Theo Kojak, as played by Telly Savalas, were his shaven head and his addiction to lollipops, which he sucked as an aid to thought.

Kojak had been 20 years on the force and had a failed marriage behind him. His beat was Manhattan's South Precinct, which he covered from his office in the 13th precinct building on 21st Street between First and Second Avenues, sometimes drinking coffee from a plastic beaker while at the wheel of his car. Like Columbo, he became a kind of folk hero, his most remembered line the salutation: 'Who loves ya, baby?'

Bobby Crocker, his aide, for whom he was always bellowing, was played by Kevin Dobson. Another of his men was the woolly-haired Detective Stavros, whose name appeared on cast lists as Demosthenes, but was later identified as George Savalas, Telly's brother.

The most glamorous of the cops of the Seventies was Sgt. Suzanne 'Pepper' Anderson in *Police Woman*, which began in 1974, a spin-off from an episode of *Police Story*, an anthology series created by Joseph Wambaugh. She was a brassy divorcee, an undercover police woman with the Criminal Conspiracy department of the Los Angeles Police Department, and was played by Angie Dickinson, frequently in short skirts and fishnet tights as she posed as a hooker or stripper.

One month before filming the first episode Dickinson went to the Hollywood Division police station with other members of the cast to absorb the atmosphere, and returned shaken. She said later:

'We walked across the street, sat down on the kerb and opened up our lunch boxes of hamburgers and french fries, then an incredibly loud series of gun bursts echoed from an undetermined source. We knew something was terribly wrong. Policemen with hand guns and shotguns began to scatter in all directions. We were ordered to take cover behind parked cars – and you can bet we did. It was a terrifying sight to look over the hood of the car and see a dozen men with guns drawn, crouched everywhere, trying to locate the unseen attacker. It was my first taste of what the law enforcement business is all about.'

In fact an unknown man had walked in through the back door of the police station and drawn a gun. Four police officers fired, killing him instantly.

Violence was growing again on television as in life, and in 1975 aggressive action and street filming were combined skilfully in Britain in *The Sweeney*. The title was a nickname for Scotland Yard's elite Flying Squad, derived from Cockney rhyming slang in which Sweeney Todd equals Squad. Traditionally, since the days of *Dixon of Dock Green*, British television had presented the police as essentially benevolent, but the characters of *The Sweeney* were not concerned with helping old ladies across streets. They were the hard men of the fight against serious crime and less inhibited than any previous British television cops.

Det. Inspector Jack Regan (John Thaw) and his Cockney sergeant, George Carter (Dennis Waterman), disobeyed orders, drank, had affairs and actually seemed to enjoy rough-houses. They were honest – up to a point. In one episode Regan was seen searching his superior's files for his own annual report. The action was filmed in the streets of London and edited slickly to provide the most exciting car chases and

Angie Dickinson as Sgt. Pepper Anderson uses a car radio to seek back-up in Police Woman.

punch-ups seen on the small screen. The dialogue was crisp and there was quirky humour. 'We're the Sweeney, son, and we ain't had our dinner yet,' Regan told a suspect.

Britain's highest-ranking policemen did not care for it. Sir David McNee, Metropolitan Police Commissioner at the time, criticised its possible influence on young officers. 'For a policeman to carry out police duty by following *The Sweeney* would be the road to disaster,' he said. However, the rank and file were not averse to being depicted in a macho light and Battersea detectives gave Thaw a silver cigarette box engraved: 'We wish all DIs were like you.'

Guns at the ready, John Thaw, Dennis Waterman and Nick Brimble in The Sweeney.

Buddies

In America, in the same year, *Starsky and Hutch* also made a feature of car chases, but more important to its success was the appeal of its two young stars. Wisecracking Dave Starsky and his more reserved partner, Ken Hutchinson, were handsome, athletic undercover policemen known jointly to the production team as 'Hutchsky'; Paul Michael Glaser and David Soul, who played them, became the heroes of men and the pin-ups of women around the world.

In Britain, Kenneth Oxford, Chief Constable of Merseyside, observed later: 'When the *Starsky and Hutch* series was showing, police on patrol duty were adopting sunglasses and wearing their gloves with the cuffs turned down. They also started driving like bloody maniacs.'

But an anti-violence crusade by churches and America's Parent Teacher Association hit the show, and action was watered down for fear of losing sponsors. Soul complained: 'As far as I'm concerned, violence is action, and if the action is good then it has every right to be in the show'. He went on:

'I directed an episode once in which a man fell five storeys to his death. "Oh no," said the network. "You can't have that. Take it out." I refused. It was an integral part of the story, and his death quite clearly was brought about by his own actions. So the network said, "OK, keep it in, but he falls only three storeys." On another occasion we were told we had too many "damns" and too many shoot-outs in one episode. Down came the ruling: we could keep a gunfight but only if we cut two "damns". It's crazy. We should just get on and make good entertainment.'

The action was replaced with larger helpings of romance and sentiment, and a greater concern for the inter-relationship between the two principals. It became a buddy series, and led inevitably in 1981 to a

American-British alliance: Dempsey and Makepeace, *played by Michael Brandon and Glynis Barber.*

Inspector Morse (John Thaw) and Detective Sergeant Lewis (Kevin Whately) puzzle over five across.

Top *Once upon a time there were three girls . . .
and they became* Charlie's Angels.

Left *Sherlock Holmes and Dr Watson on the
Baker Street set in Manchester.*

Above *The name may have changed every
week, but there's no mistaking the welcoming
portals of* Fawlty Towers.

female buddy series. This had, in fact, been planned long before, when producer Barney Rosenzweig met writer Barbara Corday (subsequently Mrs Rosenzweig). She pointed out to him: 'Through history women have always been portrayed as being one up and one down; the pretty one versus the one with the glasses. There has been no such thing as a female buddy movie or a buddy relationship between women.' And so *Cagney and Lacey* was devised as a story about two equal women in partnership. 'The police officer stuff was an excuse to get on television,' said Rosenzweig. 'Of course, it's interesting, but it's not the core of the show.'

It took Rosenzweig seven years to get it on screen. The pilot show – seen as a TV movie – starred Tyne Daly and Loretta Swit, but when it came to a series, Swit was still in the long-running *M*A*S*H*, and Meg Foster got the part; but the partnership was seen as too butch, and she was replaced after a season by Sharon Gless.

Christine Cagney (Gless) was ambitious, single, a career woman, abrasive, sometimes lonely, struggling with alcoholism, and regarded by some as promiscuous, though Corday saw her as 'a healthy, active, heterosexual female'. Mary Beth Lacey (Daly) had a husband and two young children. She came from a broken home – her father walked out and her mother died – so she had empathy for outsiders. She had undergone an illegal abortion at 19, and had survived breast cancer and a gunshot wound. On duty the two women carried .38s, drove like saloon car racers and would use any means just within the law to put villains behind bars. Off duty, one worried about what to make for supper while the other considered dating a patrolman.

An obvious next move was to team male and female cops, and it happened in 1985 in *Dempsey and Makepeace*, made in Britain but with the American market in view. Lt. Jim Dempsey was a New Yorker who had made the city too hot for himself. With corrupt police and politicians as well as organised crime seeking Dempsey's head after a drugs bust, the Police Commissioner sent him on a sabbatical until the temperature cooled. He was ordered to London to join SI10, an undercover unit formed by the Prime Minister and Home Secretary to combat major crime. Dempsey, a former soldier in Vietnam, a tough, mean survivor with a law degree, bad manners and a readiness to go for his gun, was played by American Michael Brandon. His partner, Det. Sgt. Harriet Makepeace, was a highborn English policewoman, a peer's daughter with a science degree from Cambridge. She was a skilled computer programmer, a proficient shot and a champion archer, and was played by South African-born Glynis Barber.

In part, the series concerned the relationship between the strangely matched pair, a relationship which began frostily and grew warmer, but it also seemed to set out to prove that Britain could outdo the Americans in crash-bang action. According to stunt arranger Roy Alon, the series had 'the most spectacular and dangerous stunts ever seen on television'. At least six stunt artists were hired for each shooting. Startled Londoners saw stuntman Jason White plunge 60 ft from Tower Bridge into the Thames for one episode, belly-flopping into the river and cracking a rib as he avoided collision with the bridge. For another story two stuntmen jumped from an aircraft with one parachute, an extra large canopy being used to support the two-man descent.

The Trendy and the Classic

Miami Vice brought back a two-hero team, as in *Starsky and Hutch*, mixed with the glamour of *Dynasty*. Seedily dressed undercover men who could mix with drifters were out; in were fashion-conscious yuppies, resulting in what were called television's first 'designer cops'. Ostensibly the series, which began in 1985, was about two undercover drug squad cops in Miami, Sonny Crockett (Don Johnson) an ex-football hero living on a boat with a pet alligator, and Ricardo Tubbs (Philip Michael Thomas), a black New Yorker, but its style was derived from pop music videos, with the intention of attracting young audiences.

The musical score was specially commissioned rock, the lyrics dovetailing with the story, performed by stars including Tina Turner, Phil Collins and the Rolling Stones. Clothes were from Uomo and Gianni

Versace; the casual style became known as 'the *Vice* look'. There were Porsche cabriolets and speedboats. Johnson, as Crockett, affected an unshaven jaw which was copied around the world and became known as 'designer stubble'. Daytime scenes were filmed in pastel colours, night scenes in dark hues. Every prop was colour co-ordinated. 'We were just being contemporary at a time when the rest of television was operating in the Fifties,' said Johnson.

The series was filmed on location, which initially worried Miami civic authorities, who feared that the association with drug dealing would give the area a bad name; they soon found there was no cause for their concern. Crowds flocked to Miami in the hope of seeing the stars.

The snag about trendiness is that fashions in pop music and clothes change fast and what is ahead of style at one moment can soon seem dated. That was no concern to the makers of *Inspector Morse* in 1987, for there was nothing remotely trendy about it. It was a series with no punch-ups, gun fights or car crashes. Morse was an Oxford policeman with a liking for real ale, a dislike of spending money, and a head full of Latin quotations, lines of verse and clever, though often wrong, theories. He was played by John Thaw, whom it was widely believed had said he would never play another policeman after his long and acclaimed stint as Regan in *The Sweeney*. Thaw denied this: 'I didn't say I would never play another policeman; I said I would never play another Regan. Morse is not like him in any way. He is much more laid back. He takes things coolly and calmly and uses his brain more than Regan. Morse is a much gentler man all round. Anyway he is out of condition and terrified of heights. In fact, in lots of ways he is very old fashioned, a classic British fictional detective.'

He was created by Colin Dexter, a GCE examiner in Latin, Greek, ancient history and English, and a compiler of crossword puzzles, who admitted: 'I don't know anything about police work.' However, it was not true, he said, that he had never been in a police station. He had – twice – after his bike had been stolen.

Just an old fashioned british detective. John Thaw as Inspector Morse and Kevin Whately as D. S. Lewis.

3
Sleuths
The Private Investigators

Alongside the police in crime fiction, assisting or frustrating them, there have always been private investigators, some of them professionals and others gifted amateurs. One of the earliest of television's private detectives to be internationally known was Britain's *Mark Saber*, who was remarkable for having only one arm, being played by South African-born Donald Gray, who had lost an arm in World War Two. Gray's matinee idol profile won him a big following in the USA, despite the fact that when *Saber* began in 1956 there had already been an American television hero of the same name, a policeman played by Tom Conway.

When Gray visited New York in the wake of his success, he found himself billed as 'the Englishman with too much sex appeal'. Fans greeted him at the airport carrying banners reading, 'Welcome Mark Saber'. 'Until I saw those banners I was looking round the plane to see if Johnnie Ray was aboard,' said Gray. 'It was so strange walking about in a foreign land and being recognised. A plump, jolly, coloured woman stopped me on Broadway and said jokingly, "How's it, Mark Saber; you over here to clean up our crime, honey?".'

Gray, who had earlier been one of the first postwar BBC television announcers, made 160 *Saber* adventures, with Diana Decker as his secretary, Stevie Ames, and Neil McCallum as a Canadian associate, Pete Paulson. The penalty was to find himself typecast, and he was obliged to work almost

exclusively in radio and commercials until his death in 1978.

Britain also produced the oddest of all private eye series in *Randall and Hopkirk (Deceased)* in 1972. While Jeff Randall (Mike Pratt) was flesh and blood, his partner, Marty Hopkirk (Kenneth Cope), had become a ghost, materialising and dematerialising, still earthbound and insisting on continuing the partnership. Only one man knew that Hopkirk was still on earth and that was Randall. Only one man could see him; that was Randall. Even Hopkirk's widow Jean (Annette Andre), working as Randall's secretary, could not detect his presence.

However, invisibility was a considerable asset to the agency because the ghost could walk through locked doors and could never be assaulted or arrested. Cope said of his spectral role:

'In a way mine is the easiest part of the three because I can look at the others, whereas Mike Pratt is the only other player who can look at me. But what I have to remember all the time is that I daren't touch anything, because as a ghost I would go right through it. It's natural, for instance, to lean up against a mantelshelf, but only a human can do this. The hardest thing is to know what to do with my hands.'

Hollywood Eyes

Professional private eyes are, of course, more associated with America, and *77*

Girls fell for Kookie in 77 Sunset Strip – *and also for Edd Byrnes who played him.*

Sunset Strip, which began in 1958, concerned two former government agents operating from offices on the famous two-mile stretch of shops and bars in Hollywood. The action took place mainly outside Dean Martin's restaurant, Dino's. The stars were Efrem Zimbalist Jr as Stuart Bailey, and Roger Smith as Jeff Spencer, but a minor character played by Edward (later known as Edd) Byrnes was the focus of most attention.

He was Gerald Lloyd Kookson III, or Kookie, a teenage parking lot attendant, constantly combing his glossy, ducktailed hair and speaking in what was called 'jive talk'. A glossary was issued for foreigners. Some of the phrases were:

Drum beaters – advertising men
Wheel-spinning – getting nowhere
Cut your motor – stop
Let's exitville – let's go

Keep the eyes rolling – watch out
Real nervous – good
Tintype – photo
Making the long green – earning money
Pony chaser – horse racing enthusiast
Out of print – from another town
Go the minnow route – have a fish dinner
Ride the straws – extra chips
Blast off – leave

Teenage girls went wild about Kookie. He became a regular, and was promoted to join the firm as a private eye. During more than 200 episodes Byrnes's fan mail rose from 5,000 to 10,000 letters a week, and he made a hit record, a duet with Connie Stevens, *Kookie, Kookie, Lend Me Your Comb.*

Connie Stevens was then one of the stars of *Hawaiian Eye*, which began 134 episodes in 1959. The investigators were Tracey Steele and Tom Lopaka (Anthony Eisley and Robert Conrad) who were also house detectives at the Hawaiian Village Hotel. They were aided by Cricket Blake (Stevens), a singer at the hotel and part-time photographer, and a taxi-driver named Kim (played by Poncie Ponce, a Hawaiian-born Filipino, whose name *TV Times* did not publish because the then editor thought that it sounded unpleasant).

In the Sixties and early Seventies there was a vogue for single-word titles, consisting simply of the virile name of the private eye. There was *Mannix*, who used state-of-the-art technology against crime. Joe Mannix (Mike Connors) worked for a crime-fighting organisation named Intertect, and his car was equipped with a computerised criminal information system which could transmit and receive fingerprints and photographs of suspects. There was *Banacek*, a Boston-based, self-employed insurance company detective recovering stolen merchandise for 10 per cent of its value. Thomas Banacek, hailed by the production company as 'television's first Polish-American hero', was played by George Peppard.

However, the biggest character of this era in more than one sense was *Cannon*, a high-priced detective on the west coast of America, for he was no bronzed, athletic hero but a middle-aged, 19-stone heavyweight who wheezed when he ran. In fact,

William Conrad examines a fish dinner in
Cannon – *looking as if he has already eaten.*

the series, which began in 1971, was developed for and around William Conrad, who played him, rather than by the usual process of acquiring a story and then casting a suitable actor for the leading role. Conrad cheerfully admitted the idea sounded crazy:

'For 15 years before *Cannon* I couldn't get much work as an actor because I was too fat and unattractive. I'm 53 years old, 5ft 9in tall, look like an overfed walrus, and I'm bald to boot. Producers took one look at me and ran. So I had to rely on radio. I played Matt Dillon for 11 years on the air in *Gunsmoke* and I worked in TV as a producer.'

As *Cannon* he began a new career on screen. Meanwhile new detective heroes made their debuts. *Barnaby Jones*, in 1973, was a veteran investigator played by Buddy Ebsen, who had handed over his Jones Detective Agency to his son and retired to breed horses, but his son was murdered and so he strapped on his Colt .38 in its worn leather holster and went back to work, initially to hunt down his son's killer. His assistant, his daughter-in-law, Betty, was played by Lee Meriwether, a former Miss America.

A year later David Janssen created the role of *Harry O* (for Orwell), an ex-policeman, forced to retire after being shot in the back, living in a beach shack in San Diego (and later Los Angeles) and taking occasional cases. But *Harry O* was overshadowed by the runaway success of another Californian detective who made his debut on American screens in the same week. Every episode of *The Rockford Files* opened with the sound of a telephone answering machine: 'Hello, this is James Rockford. At the sound of the tone, please leave your name and number. I'll get back to you as soon as possible.'

Jim Rockford, played by James Garner, was chief operative (and sole operative, for that matter) of the Rockford Private Detective Agency. An ex-con, having served five years for a crime of which he was innocent, he lived alone in a shabby oceanside caravan, his gun in a biscuit jar, subsisting on junk food. He was a smooth talker but still got beaten up, and usually found his clients unable to pay him. He was, like Raymond Chandler's Philip Marlowe, an honest man in a greedy, selfish, corrupt society. Noah Beery Jr played his father, Joseph (Rocky) Rockford, who stopped by to share a pizza with his son, and Joe Santos was Sgt. Dennis Becker, his pal in the police.

Garner played the role for six years before he called a halt, complaining that rolling out of moving cars, leaping from windows, and making flying tackles had damaged his knees. 'They're finished,' he said. 'Too many hours on concrete, too many falls. I've had six operations and I just can't take any more pain. The series has already made a lot of money, so who needs more? I don't. What I need is my health. I've worked six days a week and then been kept awake at night with pain.'

Glamorous Eyes

In the real world women investigators are rare, and there has certainly never been a team as stunning as *Charlie's Angels*, a sensation in 1976. The Angels were three dazzling former policewomen, employed by Charlie Townsend, the wealthy never-seen head of Townsend Investigations, Los Angeles. Every programme began with a voice-over:

'Once upon a time there were three girls who went to the police academy and they were each assigned very hazardous duties, but I took them away from all that and now they work for me. My name is Charlie.'

The voice was that of John Forsythe, later to be seen as well as heard as a star of *Dynasty*.

Charlie sent his Angels on assignments which might require feminine talents – like posing as strippers or night club singers – but arrangements were invariably made by telephone; he was always too busy with associates to meet his Angels.

The original three were Sabrina Duncan (Kate Jackson), Kelly Garrett (Jaclyn Smith) and Jill Munroe (Farrah Fawcett-Majors, later to discard the Majors after her divorce from Lee Majors, star of *The Six Million Dollar Man*). They were all flashing teeth, flowing hair and suntanned limbs. They were displayed in jeans, dresses, fun furs, shorts and bikinis – especially shorts and bikinis, while any pretext was used to show the bra-less girls in wet T-shirts. This caused the programme and imitators to be known in television as 'jiggly shows'.

In the course of stories the Angels were frequently menaced, slapped or bound – all male fantasies were catered for – but they survived without a beautiful hair out of place, merely stepping into new clothes. (The actresses sometimes made as many as a dozen quick changes a day in their three luxury caravans.) Executive producer Aaron Spelling admitted: 'We're more concerned with hairdos and gowns than the twists and turns of the plot.'

The popularity of the actresses was incredible – particularly that of Fawcett, who featured on the covers of magazines around the world as a symbol of fitness and beauty. Manufacturers queued up to woo them with contracts for endorsing cosmetics and clothes, and at one time the names of more than 300 journalists were on a waiting list for interviews, their enthusiasm inflamed by rumours of feuds and tantrums.

When the series ended in 1981 after 120 episodes, Jaclyn Smith was the sole survivor of the original trio. Cheryl Ladd, Tanya Roberts and Shelley Hack had, at different times, replaced the others. But American television is loath to relinquish a winning formula and seven years later *Angels 88* was in production with a team of four new girls chosen from 20,000 applications for the parts.

Aaron Spelling, who made *Charlie's Angels*, was also responsible in 1979 for *Hart to Hart*, an updating of the sophisticated and witty *Thin Man* films of the Thirties which starred William Powell and Myrna Loy as Nick and Nora Charles. Robert Wagner and Stefanie Powers played Jonathan and Jennifer Hart, a wealthy businessman and his journalist wife with the time and money to indulge their whim of playing at being private detectives, which

James Garner clearly has the upper hand for once in The Rockford Files.

Lionel Stander, Stefanie Powers and Robert Wagner (with dog Freeway) in Hart to Hart.

gave them an excuse for flying to exotic locations.

The hero of *Magnum* in 1980 already lived in one – enjoying a champagne existence on a beer income. Thomas Sullivan Magnum, known as TS to his friends, was a retired Naval intelligence officer who became a private investigator in Hawaii, living rent-free in a beach house with the use of swimming pool and Ferrari in return for guarding them on behalf of their playboy owner, a wealthy writer. When not working, Magnum (Tom Selleck) was often to be found at Rick's place, an updated version of Rick's in *Casablanca*.

Glamour was introduced into the world of crime in a different way in *Moonlighting*, in 1985, by casting Cybill Shepherd as Maddie Hayes, an international model, who, swindled by her advisers, found herself the owner of the Blue Moon Detective Agency in Los Angeles. Rather than selling it, she decided to team up with its operative, the chauvinistic David Addison (Bruce Willis). An edgy romance then developed between them, with her cold and professional, him wisecracking, for *Moonlighting* was more a romantic comedy than a crime series. It was the chemistry between the two stars and the fast, compressed dialogue (which caused scripts to be twice as long as the average) that made it a big hit.

The Spinster and the Widow

Perhaps the most surprising popularity in the 1980s was that of numerous investigators created decades earlier by Dame Agatha Christie, who died in 1976. Thames Television's *The Agatha Christie Hour*, and the BBC's *Spider's Web* in 1982 were followed by LWT's *Partners in Crime* in 1983, and many American and British TV movies, but the most notable success was that of the BBC's *Miss Marple* series which began in 1984.

Joan Hickson starred as the spinster from the village of St Mary Mead who could solve crimes quicker than the police. She was 78 when she embarked on the role of Jane Marple, 38 years after she had played another spinster in one of Christie's plays on the London stage and received a congratulatory letter from the writer with a post-script that said: 'I hope some day you will play my dear Miss Marple'. Hickson forgot about it until after she had accepted the role. 'I didn't think I was right at all – not thin and small enough – but I decided to have a bash. Then my daughter found that letter again in my desk and it was, well, a bit heartening. I do hope the dear thing, wherever she may happen to be, is pleased.'

As Jane Marple, Hickson adopted lace-up shoes, sensible tweeds and a felt hat, and carried a crocodile handbag, though the piercing blue eyes were her own. The stories, set in the Thirties and Forties in drawing rooms and libraries in Queen Anne houses in the Home Counties, were populated by butlers and parlourmaids, retired colonels and plodding policemen. The programmes sold among other places to China. 'What can they be making of Miss Marple in China?' wondered Hickson, understandably. 'People do have such definite ideas about her. I think she's rather a small, birdy lady who is totally unobtrusive. You'd pass her in the village street but she knows everything that is going on. . . .'

Coincidentally, in the same year, America produced *Murder, She Wrote*, the creation of writer-producer Peter Fischer, about a middle-aged woman investigator, played by Angela Lansbury, who was born in England but settled in America during World War Two. Lansbury, who was nudging 60 when the series was first seen, played Jessica Fletcher, a genteel, bicycling widow living in a Victorian house in Cabot Cove, Maine, a writer of best-selling whodunnits that had begun with *The Corpse Danced at Midnight*. After solving two murders when a relative was arrested as a suspect, in order to clear him, she continued to write and solve crimes, with the help of a chain of relatives across the country.

The whimsical series made Jessica Fletcher a heroine with middle-class women who liked the way she did her hair and make-up and dealt with men.

Classic American, Classic English

No one could have been further from the worlds of Jane Marple and Jessica Fletcher than *Mike Hammer*, Mickey Spillane's tough private eye, originally played on television in 1958 by Darren McGavin, but in 1983 by Stacy Keach after a successful two-hour movie, *Murder Me, Murder You*. Keach had always wanted to play Hammer:

'I guess it's just the ham in me. This Mike Hammer has something for everyone. He's tough, charming and romantic – the classic American detective. What makes him different from all the other guys is the way he expresses himself. Mickey Spillane is a street poet and has permeated Hammer's language with that quality.'

After 24 episodes production ended when Keach was jailed for possessing cocaine while on a visit to England. 'Hammer in the Slammer', ran one newspaper headline. Keach left Reading jail out of work, but was back as Hammer in 1986.

Hammer, of course, epitomises the wise-cracking, womanising American private eye, but the most famous detective in fiction remains England's Sherlock Holmes, who used observation and deduction rather than muscles. Sir Arthur Conan Doyle's great detective had been the hero of many films and television series, but the definitive Holmes, in the opinion of many devotees, arrived only in 1984 in *The Adventures of Sherlock Holmes*.

For the series Granada Television built a Victorian Baker Street, or, at least, the neighbourhood of 221B, close by their permanent, outdoor *Coronation Street* set in Manchester. Jeremy Brett played Holmes, with saturnine glances and cold command, and with all the props – pipe, magnifying glass, cocaine syringe and violin. He shed a stone in weight to resemble the gaunt Holmes of popular image, grew his hair long and gelled it to his skull. David Burke (and Edward Hardwicke, who succeeded him) played Dr Watson as a more intelligent ally than earlier actors had done.

'I see Holmes as someone who's always been alone, neglected by his parents, brought up by a cruel nurse, friendless at school,' said Brett. 'Maybe he once loved a girl who never took any notice of him. He needs Watson but he can't say thank you, he can't ask for help, he's starved of affection.'

In episode 13, *The Final Problem*, Holmes appeared to meet his death in a struggle with his enemy, Moriarty, at the Reichenbach Falls. It was the first time a film or television company had used the actual location in the Swiss Alps where Doyle set the story. Filming began with Brett as Holmes, and Eric Porter as Moriarty, locked in a struggle at the cliff edge, then stunt men Mark Boyle (as Holmes) and Alf Joint (as Moriarty) replaced them in identical clothing for the 400-ft fall. The two tiny figures were seen plummeting towards the white water; what viewers did not see was how their descents were arrested by steel cables to allow them to land on rough ground at the cliff foot.

Granada then brought Holmes back for a further series, *The Return of Sherlock Holmes* in a story called *The Empty House*. 'Just as Conan Doyle was forced by public pressure to bring back Holmes after his disappearance at Reichenbach, so we have decided to go ahead and make more stories for the viewers,' said producer Michael Cox.

The series has been sold to more than 60 countries, including Japan, which buys few programmes from abroad. Holmes, however, acquired a cult following there, and at one time Brett was receiving 1,000 fan letters a week from Japan.

The End . . . or is it? Holmes (Jeremy Brett) and Moriarty (Eric Porter) struggle for supremacy.

4
Ways of Making You Laugh
Situation Comedies

Situation comedies have long been the mainstay of television, and most of them have been about the frictions in family life. The pattern was set as early as 1951 when *I Love Lucy* began, with Lucille Ball as Lucy Ricardo (née McGillicuddy), well-meaning and lovable, but scatterbrained and childlike. Striving to be a supportive wife, while yearning for a career in show business, Lucy taxed the patience of her Cuban bandleader husband, Ricky (played by Ball's husband, Cuban bandleader Desi Arnez), and their New York apartment neighbours, Fred and Ethel Mertz (William Frawley and Vivian Vance).

Typical episodes involved Lucy getting the idea Ricky was plotting to kill her, Lucy trying to be a pal to her husband by joining him in a poker game, Lucy trying to lose 12 pounds to break into show business, Lucy getting on a quiz show, and Lucy dividing the living room in half in a bid to persuade Ricky to be tidy around the house.

Ball's own pregnancy in 1953, when she gave birth to Desi Jr, was written into the stories, and the Ricardos became an established part of American life. An estate agent in Connecticut, offering a furnished cottage to rent, chose as a selling point, 'a cocktail table that is a replica of the one in *I Love Lucy*'. The Marshall Field department store in Chicago began closing an hour earlier on Mondays so that customers and staff could get home in time to watch the show. A parent-teacher association in Lynn, Mass.,

demanded the local station screen the programme earlier so that children could be got to bed. A Lions Club in Santa Barbara, California bought a TV set and adjourned meetings for half an hour at programme time to draw members.

Lucille Ball had always had to fight — as a model, a salesgirl, a waitress, a bit-part player, a Goldwyn Girl and a radio comedienne. She had been in 70 movies, but had not achieved real stardom. That came at 40 when she turned to TV. On television she and her husband were in charge. They pioneered filming before a studio audience, ensuring preservation of the shows, and through their company, Desilu, they controlled distribution and rights. In a few years Desilu was a giant, owning the RKO studios where they were once under contract.

Their marriage had struck rocks some years before the show started, and Ball had begun divorce proceedings, but they were reconciled and had a second wedding in church. They claimed the series had solidified their marital happiness. When they had a row one would turn to the other and say, 'You know, this would make a perfect episode for *Lucy*,' and they would start to discuss the script. However, this stratagem did not work indefinitely. In 1960, after 179 episodes of *I Love Lucy*, they were divorced and Arnaz sold his share of their company to Ball.

The next year she began 155 episodes of *The Lucy Show* as Lucy Carmichael,

America's greatest female clown, Lucille Ball, fools with a saxophone in I Love Lucy.

widowed mother of two, in Connecticut, followed in 1968 by the first of 144 episodes of *Here's Lucy* in which she played Lucille Carter, again a widow but a secretary in California. Her children, Lucie Arnaz and Desi Arnaz Jr, appeared as Kim and Craig Carter, the children of her television character. *Here's Lucy* continued in production until 1974, by which time, with new shows and repeats, Ball had never been off screen

for 23 years. It was commonplace for there to be four or five showings of *Lucy* programmes on a single day in New York in the Seventies, and they were also being seen around the world. *I Love Lucy* had been the first American situation comedy seen in Britain; it began in ITV's opening week in

1955 as the highlight of Sunday night viewing, and Ball's picture was on the cover of the first issue of *TV Times*. It was only in 1986 when she launched *Life with Lucy* at the age of 75 that her formula failed.

Ball's opposite number, the leading male star of domestic situation comedy in the Sixties, was Dick Van Dyke, who made 158 episodes of *The Dick Van Dyke Show* as Rob Petrie, head writer of *The Alan Brady Show*, living in New York, with his ex-dancer wife Laura (Mary Tyler Moore) and their son Richie. Van Dyke was bright and breezy with smiling charm. He once described himself as 'the male Julie Andrews', but off-screen he had a drink problem, about which he went public in the Seventies, making films for Alcoholics Anonymous.

Even so, he managed to fit in movies, including *Mary Poppins*, while making the series, which ran from 1961 to 1966 and continued to be repeated long afterwards.

Togetherness is all. Mary Tyler Moore and Dick Van Dyke share a sweater in his show.

One reason for its enduring popularity, advanced by Van Dyke, was that slang of the day was banned from the scripts, so the dialogue did not date. He returned with *The New Dick Van Dyke Show* in 1971 playing Dick Preston, host of a chat show.

Meanwhile the slim, mobile-faced Mary Tyler Moore, who had won two Emmy Awards as best actress playing Laura Petrie, had begun a formula-breaking series of her own. Series like Van Dyke's were known in television as 'Hi, honey, I'm home' shows, because they followed the convention that the husband went out to work and the wife waited at home for him and did the domestic chores. *The Mary Tyler Moore Show*, which began in 1970, was different because she was seen as a career woman. Mary Richards was a reporter in the news room of a Minneapolis TV station, a single woman in her thirties, who fared quite well on her own, but had love affairs. The series was regarded as even more daring because Minneapolis was not seen as glamorous, and the producers insisted on filming before a live audience and not dubbing laughter from a tape, which was a common practice to save time.

The first ratings were low, but then they climbed. The series was polished and intelligent. It was credited with turning situation comedy into art, and it also changed the television image of women. Mary Tyler Moore Enterprises, founded by Moore and her husband, Grant Tinker, sold the syndication rights for millions. When the series ended after seven years it was not because of sagging ratings; Moore decided to leave on a high note and move on to other challenges.

Several characters from *The MTM Show* had already been given their own spin-off series. *Rhoda* followed husband-hunting Rhoda Morganstern (Valerie Harper) to New York; *Phyllis* followed widowed landlady Phyllis Lindstrom (Cloris Leachman) to San Francisco, and *Lou Grant* showed the sacked Minneapolis TV news director (Edward Asner) in more serious adventures as city editor of a daily paper in Los Angeles.

Bizarre Families

In the Sixties domestic sitcoms presented increasingly bizarre characters. *The Beverly*

Mary Tyler Moore introduces a Christmas note into the newsroom in her series.

Hillbillies were mountain folk from the Ozarks who struck oil and moved to fashionable Beverly Hills, travelling on an old flatbed truck loaded with jugs of corn liquor and 25 million dollars. The Clampett family consisted of Jed (Buddy Ebsen), a widower; Elly May (Donna Douglas), his buxom, guileless daughter; 'Granny' Daisy Moses (Irene Ryan), his crotchety mother-in-law, with enough wrinkles for several grandmothers – her make up sessions took

almost two hours every morning – and Jethro Bodine (Max Baer, son of the former world heavyweight boxing champion), his tall, dark, handsome, ox-like nephew.

The comedy was based on their remaining unchanged by their new circumstances. So Granny tried to buy from food stores such staples of her recipes as 'possum innards', dried beetles and lizards' eggs, and was admonished by the local doctor for practising mountain remedies and polluting the atmosphere by making evil-smelling lye soap. The dialogue was on a par. A banker's son calling on Jed's daughter asked, 'Is Elly

May ready?' and Granny answered: 'She sure is. She's been ready since she was 14.'

Some critics accused the show of perpetuating offensive hillbilly stereotypes; others saw it as satirising money-orientated Beverly Hills. Ebsen's view was:

'If the show has any overtones, any message, it's that people have more than they need in the material world. Our social comment is that people should live simpler – not necessarily like the Clampetts, but simpler.'

Most journalists panned the series. 'At no time does it give the viewer credit for even a smattering of intelligence,' said *Variety*. Most viewers adored it. Donna Douglas, who, as Elly May, popularised dungarees for girls, received 100 proposals a week. President Nixon told Irene Ryan in 1970: 'We love your show. Anytime we get a chance to look at it, we do.' In Britain and Japan it broke records for American series. More than 200 programmes were made over nine years.

After hillbillies came witches. *Bewitched* introduced pretty Samantha Stevens, who shocked her ad-man husband Darrin on their wedding night by confessing to being a witch; he begged her to stop using her powers, and she tried, but sometimes the challenge to employ them was too great. She could make a flower bloom, or clean a room in an instant merely by wrinkling her nose.

Samantha was played by Elizabeth Montgomery, daughter of Robert, though she had not sought television stardom; she took on the role in order to work with her husband, William Asher, who directed the first 14 episodes in 1964. Darrin was played by Dick York until 1969 when he was replaced by Dick Sargent, although no announcement was made; the face simply changed – as if by witchcraft.

Another star of the series, though an unseen one, was special effects man Dick Albain, who invented for Samantha's use a 'magic' self-operating vacuum cleaner (which was actually remotely controlled) and suitcases that packed and unpacked themselves (when invisible wires were pulled). When objects had to be dematerialised in Samantha's hand, Montgomery would freeze, Albain would remove the

The Beverly Hillbillies: *Buddy Ebsen, Irene Ryan, Max Baer and Donna Douglas.*

object and the footage of Albain would later be cut away. Montgomery said:

'It took a lot of practice before I learned how to hold my hands perfectly still, but that was easier than a scene in which I was supposed to clean the kitchen by witchcraft. I sort of went "Swoosh" with my arms raised, then had to leave them up in the air, aching, while the crew swept and dusted to get the kitchen immaculate before the scene resumed.'

The number of witches in the series doubled when Darrin and Samantha became the parents of Tabitha, who was initially played in different scenes by identical twins – a not uncommon practice in television, where the hours of work of small children are strictly regulated. (In a 1977 spin-off, *Tabitha*, she was seen as grown up and working for a TV chat show host, and was played by Lisa Hartman.) The witches' numbers were further increased when they were joined by Samantha's mother, Endora

(Agnes Moorehead), who cast spells on Darrin when he annoyed her, Samantha's mischievous lookalike cousin Serena (who was also played by Montgomery) and finally another Stevens child, Adam, who was a warlock.

The witches of *Bewitched* were attractive supernaturals, but 1964 also brought two families of grotesques. *The Addams Family* was based on the macabre work of *New Yorker* cartoonist Charles Addams, and the family included Gomez (John Astin), a lawyer who kept a pet octopus named Aristotle; his lovely wife Morticia (Carolyn Jones) who cultivated an African Strangler, a man-eating plant; son Pugsley (Ken Weatherwax) who kept a gallows and an electric chair in his playroom; daughter Wednesday (Lisa Loring) who played with a headless doll and a black widow spider named Homer; and shaven-headed Uncle Fester (veteran star Jackie Coogan), who lit electric light bulbs by putting them in his mouth. They were served by Lurch, a 6 ft 9 in harpsichord-playing butler (Ted Cassidy), who entered rooms with the inquiry: 'You rannnnng?' But the family did not think they were odd; it was the people in the world outside who were strange.

Their rivals, *The Munsters*, were ghouls. Herman Munster (6 ft 7 in Fred Gwynne), a funeral director, was Frankenstein's monster, with a bolt through his neck. Although the series was shot in black and white, he wore green make-up, while his wife Lily (Yvonne De Carlo), a vampire, had a chalk-white face and fiendish fingernails. Their son Eddie (Butch Patrick), a werewolf, had pointed ears, and Grandpa (Al Lewis) was a mad, 378-year-old Dracula-like scientist who drove a 160 mph coffin on wheels and could change into a bat.

Both series were in production for two years, *The Addams Family* running to 64 programmes, and *The Munsters* to 70.

Fifties Nostalgia

There was a vogue for nostalgia in the Seventies, and *American Graffiti*, the film about students in the early Sixties, inspired *Happy Days*, a television series about teen-

The Munsters: *Butch Patrick, Yvonne De Carlo, Fred Gwynne, Al Lewis and Pat Priest.*

The Fonz (in striped shirt) and friends meet the army in Happy Days.

agers in the pre-moonwalk days of the late Fifties. It set out to recreate American life in the Eisenhower era as experienced in Milwaukee by the shy, naive Richie Cunningham (Ron Howard) and his world-wise friend Warren 'Potsie' Weber (Anson Williams), students at Jefferson High School and later the University of Wisconsin.

When it began in 1974 it centred on the Cunningham home and family, but then it became apparent that another character was emerging as the most magnetic — not un-common in a television series. This was Arthur Fonzarelli, otherwise the Fonz, played by Henry Winkler. He was a college drop-out, a cool, self-assured operator with the girls. He rode a motorcycle, wore a black leather jacket, and had slicked-back, duck-tailed hair. The problem for the scriptwriters was that he was a loner, on the fringe, so in 1975 the show was changed to bring him to the fore. The first step was for the Fonz to rent an attic over the Cunningham garage. 'I knew that if I got him over the garage I could get him into the kitchen and he could become a member of the family,' said creator Garry Marshall. The Fonz became a folk hero, and his popularity was such that

Pepsi-Cola made a commercial starring a Fonz lookalike. A London psychiatrist explained:

'The Fonz has got as much street savvy as Starsky and Hutch or Kojak, but he is younger and groovier. He may look mean and moody but he is really a boy any mum would like. So kids can identify with him and parents approve of the character be-cause, unlike other TV heroes, the Fonz never gets into any rough stuff. Basically, the message in *Happy Days* is a very moral one.'

It ran 11 years through 255 episodes, during which time in real life Winkler married and became a father, and there were three spin-offs: *Laverne and Shirley*, *Mork and Mindy* and *Joanie Loves Chachi*.

Outrageous Families

Mary Hartman, Mary Hartman, a 1976 spoof of American daytime soaps, featured a housewife heroine (played by Louise Lasser) who reacted with the same amount of concern to a yellow, waxy build-up on her kitchen floor as the news that a family of

Hawkeye (Alan Alda) at the wheel of a jeep, with fellow members of the M∗A∗S∗H unit.

A Praying Mantis: one of the many stars of The Living Planet.

Overleaf *Edward Fox and Cynthia Harris as* Edward and Mrs Simpson.

five in the neighbourhood had been massacred. *Mary Hartman* was not an international hit, but it prepared the way for the even more outrageous *Soap*, created by Susan Harris a year later, which was.

Soap concerned the families of two sisters, one rich, one poor. The older sister was Jessica Tate (Cathryn Damon), who had an affair with a step-nephew and faced trial for his murder, but was acquitted when her crooked stockbroker husband, Chester, confessed. Careless brain surgery subsequently transformed Chester into a madman. One of their daughters, Eunice, fell in love with a professional killer, the other, Corinne, with her mother's lovers. Jessica's father, 'the major', wore uniform and was still living in World War Two. Their sardonic black butler Benson (Robert Guillaume) insulted everyone and refused to cook anything he did not like himself. (In *Benson*, a spin-off

A marital problem for Burt Campbell (Richard Mulligan) and wife Mary (Cathryn Damon) in Soap.

in 1979, he went back to buttle for the state governor.

The younger sister was Mary Campbell (Katherine Helmond), whose second husband, Burt, was for a time replaced on earth by an alien who inhabited his body while Burt was carried off in a spacecraft. One of their sons had a shotgun marriage to a Mafia boss's daughter, another was homosexual, and the third a ventriloquist who insisted on his dummy being treated as an equal.

The plots involved terminal illness, homosexuality, racism, insanity, transvestism, adultery, and sex therapy, and guyed both liberal and reactionary views. A typical *Soap* joke had Mary Campbell surprising her gay son while he was trying on her clothes. She said: 'I've told you a hundred times, that dress fastens at the back.' Churches called for the show to be banned. They complained it was immoral, debasing family life, and condemned it as a prolonged dirty joke. Others claimed it had a wild innocence. It

ran to 80 programmes over four years.

In 1985 Susan Harris followed *Soap* with *The Golden Girls*, about four middle-aged to elderly women sharing a house together. They were played by four actresses aged from 52 to 64. Rose (Betty White) was a rambling widow, Blanche (Rue Mc-Clanahan), a man-mad Southern widow who took mouth to mouth resuscitation classes because she liked kissing, Dorothy (Bea Arthur), an acerbic divorcee who had never forgiven her ex for leaving her for an air hostess after 38 years of marriage, and Sophia (Estelle Getty), Dorothy's 80-year-old mother who made outrageous remarks which were excused as an after effect of her stroke. (Once when Sophia was sleeping Dorothy held a mirror to her mouth, explaining, 'You never can tell.')

They looked like anyone's twittery, favourite aunts or grandmothers, but they discussed dating midgets, drooping breasts, incontinence, flatulence, abortion, and hot

Cliff Huxtable (Bill Cosby), wife Clair (Phylicia Rashad) and their children in The Cosby Show.

flushes. 'Probably if young actresses discussed taboo subjects the way we do the show would be bleeped,' said Betty White. 'They'd be accused of doing it for shock value, but we four ladies have been round the Horn several times.'

Susan Harris said: 'Before now a woman's worth was tied into what she looked like. At 82 Cary Grant could still have been a romantic lead, but on television a woman over 50 was cast as an axe-murderer. It's so rare you see leading ladies on TV older than 35. *The Golden Girls* reinforces that there is life after 50; people can be attractive and energetic and have romances.'

Black and Middle-Class

Bill Cosby had made a breakthrough when he co-starred with Robert Culp as a secret agent in *I Spy* in 1965 by becoming the first black actor to win equal star billing in a series, and he made more television history leading an all-black cast in *The Cosby Show* in 1984. Earlier American comedies about blacks had tended to stereotype adults as servants and clowns, and children as cute. *The Cosby Show* was the first to concern a middle-class black family.

Cliff Huxtable (played by Cosby), a New York obstetrician, and his wife Clair (Phylicia Rashad), a lawyer, were raising five children. The family, in fact, resembled Cosby's own; he kept photos of his four daughters and son in his dressing room. There were no jokes about race. Cosby detested them, and it was not a gag show. It merely dramatised small domestic crises such as the death of a pet goldfish, and the children were endearing but not cute.

Coretta Scott King, widow of Martin Luther King, said: 'The show is certainly the most positive portrayal of black family life that has ever been broadcast. With one out of three black families living below the poverty line it is inspiring to see a black family that has managed to escape the violence of poverty through education and unity.'

The series, of which Cosby was not only the star but co-creator, co-producer, and co-writer of the theme song, helped make him America's highest paid entertainer, the owner of a private jet and 15 cars including

Sgt. Bilko (Phil Silvers) enlists fellow soldiers in another get-rich-quick scheme.

a Rolls-Royce and an Aston-Martin. (Additional money came from records, films, nightclub performances and advertising.)

The Cosby Show was not without critics. Some argued that it idealised black life and ignored discrimination and poverty, but Harvard psychiatrist Dr Alvin Poussaint, a consultant on the programme whom Cosby telephoned weekly for his views, replied: 'This show is changing the white community's perspective of black Americans. It's doing far more to instill positive racial attitudes than if Bill came at the viewer with a sledgehammer or a sermon.'

In the Army

The family background has remained the classic situation comedy format, though sitcoms have also been set in all manner of other communities. The army yielded two of the greatest American series. The first was called *You'll Never Get Rich* when it began in 1955, but is now better known by other titles under which it was sold around the world: *Sgt. Bilko* and *The Phil Silvers Show*. Silvers appeared as Master Sgt. Ernest Bilko, a con artist in charge of the transport pool at an army base in Kansas. He was dedicated to the pursuit of money and manipulating the army system to acquire it. 'Men, this is it. Get your hips fitted for Jaguars,' he would exult, eyes glinting behind his glasses, when he thought he had hit upon a foolproof moneymaking scheme.

Caught up in his machinations was a rare collection of eccentrics including Mess Sgt. Rupbert Ritzik (Joe E. Ross), a dim-witted compulsive gambler, Pte. Duane Doberman (Maurice Gosfield), a cheerful simpleton, Pte. Fender (Herbie Faye), a confirmed pessimist, and Col. John 'Melonhead' Hall (Paul Ford), the commanding officer, trying unsuccessfully to make them into soldiers.

Created by Nat Hiken, the series employed talented writers, including Neil Simon, and the lines were delivered at machine-gun pace. One episode in particular, *The Court Martial*, about a chimpanzee inducted into the army by mistake, has been acclaimed a classic satire on bureaucracy. There were 138 episodes over four years, but *The New Phil Silvers Show* in 1963, in which he was cast as a similarly avaricious factory fore-man, was a flop; however, the original series was still being repeated in Britain and elsewhere when Silvers died in 1985.

The other great army series, *M*A*S*H*, was in a class of its own. It ran a phenomenal 11 years, which was three times longer than the event around which it was set – the Korean War of 1950–53. That war, how-ever, was a metaphor for Vietnam, where Americans were fighting when the series began in 1972, in the wake of a successful movie with the same title but a different cast.

The title was an acronym for the 4077th Mobile Army Surgical Hospital, and the series was set in its hutted operating theatre, wards and living quarters, the leading characters being two surgeons, originally Captains Benjamin Franklin 'Hawkeye' Pierce (Alan Alda) and 'Trapper John' McIntyre (Wayne Rogers) who was later replaced by Capt. B. J. Hunnicutt (Mike Farrell). (A spin-off series, *Trapper John MD* followed the further career of McIntyre in an American hospital, when he was played by Pernell Roberts from *Bonanza*.) Other leading characters included the Commanding Officer, Col. Henry Blake (McLean Stevenson), later replaced by Col. Sherman Potter (Harry Morgan), chief nurse

Major Margaret 'Hot Lips' Houlihan (Loretta Swit), and Cpl. Max Klinger (Jamie Farr), a clerk who wore women's clothes in an attempt to win his discharge.

The theme was the irony of doctors and nurses working, often until they dropped, to repair the damage done by armies in order to return men to the front lines, and the series did not shirk dealing with horrifying injuries. It also satirised the bureaucracy and incompetence of the military machine. The surgeons took refuge in wisecracks and jokes as they worked under primitive con-ditions at what they termed 'meatball sur-gery', and the humour was often bitter and sometimes ferocious. Most of the episodes were shot in black and white to give a period flavour.

M*A*S*H ended finally in a collective suicide pact, when re-runs were playing to 224 million people around the world. In 1982 key members of the cast had voted four to three to end the series, but were persuaded to continue. A year later their decision was unanimous. Producer Burt Metcalfe said:

'We wanted to stop while we were still doing well commercially and aesthetically, and while we still had pride and a sense of accomplishment. We had simply run out of historical anecdotes. I had interviewed more than 200 veterans of the Korean war, but once their stories ran out – as much as I hate to admit it – we were being reduced to dealing with situation comedy clichés like forgotten birthdays and anniversaries.'

The series ended in style with a two and a half hour episode, *Goodbye, Farewell and Amen*, which was seen by 125 million people in America alone. It was the last of 251 award-laden episodes. 'It had to end sometime,' said Alan Alda, who had himself won awards in three different categories – as an actor, a writer and a director. 'This is a very emotional time. We all loved the characters and the stories.'

A more conventional British medical sit-com was *Doctor in the House*, inspired by the humorous book of that title written 20 years earlier by Richard Gordon to pay for a holiday when he was newly qualified as a doctor. The television series in 1969 followed films starring Dirk Bogarde as Simon

Sparrow, a medical student at St Swithin's Hospital, but in the series Sparrow and his contemporaries had moved on and there were new students, notably Michael Upton (Barry Evans). The series led to *Doctor at Sea*, *Doctor at Large* and *Doctor on the Go*, with 138 episodes in all, over five years. In America, where stations were more prudish than in Britain, expletives were bleeped, which the actors thought made them appear to have hiccups.

Bus Driver and Hotelier

Another cheerfully vulgar British sitcom in 1969 concerned employees of a bus company. Writers Ronald Wolfe and Ronald Chesney had been invited to suggest a new comedy series, after writing *The Rag Trade*, set in a garment factory, and *Meet the Wife*, in a working class family home. They decided to devise a show which combined situations at work and repercussions at home, and *On the Buses* was because, they said, when you see a man in a busman's uniform you automatically know an awful lot about him . . . how much he earns and the sort of house he might live in.

Medical students with a skeletal assistant in Doctor in the House.

Reg Varney starred as bus driver Stan Butler, with Bob Grant as his conductor, and Stephen Lewis as a vexed Inspector. ('I *hate* you, Butler,' he cried.) Cicely Court-neidge (and later Doris Hare) played Butler's widowed mother, Anna Karen his homely sister, and Michael Robbins his idle brother-in-law. The bus – usually shown as a number 11 to the cemetery gates – was driven by Varney himself, although he was not allowed to carry fare-paying passengers. Nevertheless, whenever the television crew put up a dummy request stop in the streets there would soon be a queue of would-be passengers trying to board.

A bus depot at London's Wood Green provided the exterior of the headquarters of the Luxton Bus Company; the interior of the garage was reproduced in the studio, but whenever a bus was driven in the actors and cameramen were nearly asphyxiated by exhaust fumes, so a long pipe had to be rigged from the back of the bus to carry the gases away. Then the weight of the buses

53

Stephen Lewis as inspector, Bob Grant and Reg Varney as bus crew in On the Buses.

began distorting the floor covering and interfering with the smooth movement of cameras, so blockboard had to be laid down, after which more than 60 episodes were completed.

Fawlty Towers (1975) ran to less than a quarter of that number, but was a huge success. Written by John Cleese and his then wife, American actress Connie Booth, it was set in a terrible West Country hotel modelled on one in Torquay at which they had stayed. When they were there, the owner rebuked one guest for using his knife and fork in the American manner – the guest was, in fact, American – and threw another's briefcase out of the hotel, declaring that it probably contained a bomb. Cleese said:

'The owner was the most wonderfully rude man I've ever met. He maintained the guests stopped him from running his hotel. It was the first time we'd come across such a situation. Now we know it happens all round the world. Everybody knows somebody who acts like Basil Fawlty when under pressure.'

Cleese himself played the manic, blustering hotelier Basil Fawlty; Prunella Scales his domineering wife Sybil; and Connie Booth the pert maid, Polly, the most sensible person in the hotel – sometimes, it seemed,

the only one. Andrew Sachs was seen as a Spanish waiter, Manuel, the butt of Fawlty's bullying. Manuel's usual response to any instruction was '*Que?*', whereupon Fawlty would explain to guests: 'You'll have to excuse him – he comes from Barcelona.' Because of this, it surprised the BBC when Spanish television bought the series, but the Spanish avoided offending their viewers by transforming Manuel into an Italian when the dialogue was dubbed.

Only 13 episodes were made, one of the briefest of successful sitcoms, because, Cleese explained: 'We spent an age getting the storylines right before writing a line of dialogue. Each episode took six weeks to write and another week to rehearse and record. It was an enormous strain because it ate up the whole year on just six episodes.' But then comedy is widely regarded in television as the most difficult form of entertainment. The public demand novelty and remain loyal to the familiar. No other departments devise so many new series and in no other sector of television is the failure rate so high.

5
Creatures Great and Small

Wildlife Programmes

Alan Root is minus an index finger which surgeons had to remove after he was bitten by a puff adder. He has been mauled by a leopard, and a hippo savaged one of his legs so badly he claims: 'You could have put a Coke bottle in the hole.' Root is one of the exclusively small band of naturalist cameramen who make wildlife programmes for television – in his case for Britain's *Survival* series.

His home is a lakeside house surrounded by 80 acres of farmland in Kenya, but he and his wife, Joan, spend most of their time in the bush, flying off in their four-seat Cessna from an airstrip beside the house or driving out in their well-equipped Range Rover. For one programme he filmed the great wildebeest migration on the Serengeti plains of Tanzania while drifting over the herds of animals in a hot-air balloon. For another he captured a deadly black-necked cobra with his hands and then filmed a remarkable slow-motion sequence of it spitting venom at Joan, which was risky, particularly for him, because he knew from experience with puff adders that his body is allergic to anti-venom serum. But then he admits to being 'a stimulus addict'. He says: 'I relish situations where danger and fear are finely balanced; a project isn't interesting unless the odds are against it'.

Millions of viewers have seen his work because wildlife programmes break down barriers of viewer resistance. While sport and cop shows have their fans there are also many who loathe them, but no one seems to dislike natural history programmes.

Survival is the longest running. Its 400 programmes – still being added to – have been seen all over the world, collecting 60 international awards, grossing £15 million in foreign sales and winning the production company a Queen's Award to Industry. In America they have been introduced by John Forsythe (Blake Carrington in *Dynasty*). When two programmes were sold to China in 1979 – the first British TV programmes ever bought by the Chinese – it brought the number of countries to which *Survival* has been sold to 96, and it has since risen to 104.

The first programme in 1961 was a modest one about wildlife in central London. It opened with crashing cars and then cut to a rainy night in Hampstead where, through a car windscreen, a scavenging fox was seen sneaking into the darkness. Film followed of owls, hawks, peregrine falcons, pigeons, sparrows, mice and fish, even a puffin. One such bird had been sighted recently on the steps of the Savoy Hotel, though producer Aubrey (now Lord) Buxton, who spoke the commentary beside the lake in St James's Park and on an overgrown bomb site in the city, admits that the puffin seen in the programme was not filmed in London.

The second programme featured avocets, rare wading birds, in Suffolk. Then the small team became more ambitious. The authorities in Uganda were planning to round up the score or so remaining white rhino in the country and move them 200 miles south into Murchison Falls National Park to preserve them from hunters. The rhino were being poached out of existence for the 10 lb or more of horn carried on their snouts, this being smuggled to the Far East where it was ground to powder and sold to those who believed it to be a drug which increased sexual potency.

Buxton bought exclusive rights to film the round-up, and his team returned with exciting film. The rhino, weighing up to three tons and running at 25 mph, were lassoed from a speeding truck. A trapper wielded a bamboo pole with a noose at the end to slip over a rhino's horn; when he succeeded, the beast would charge the truck, the force of the impact lifting it on its wheels, until eventually the rhino was tethered and its legs hobbled.

From this time on *Survival* ranged the world. Buxton demanded programmes that were taut and dramatic, from which viewers could learn something but, above all, be entertained. *Survival* films were designed to be popular. They had specially scored music, much of it composed by John Dankworth. They used popular narrators, including film stars, among them Henry Fonda, James Mason, David Niven, Peter Ustinov, Orson Welles and Richard Widmark. (Buxton had decided that it was unnecessary for the presenter to continue to appear on screen.)

The programmes were not scientific films, although advice was taken from scientists during the writing of the scripts. On the other hand, they were unsentimental. Animals shown did not have to be cuddly or cute, though some were. Others were scavengers and killers, and the programme showed nature at its most raw when it was justified. The basic theme was the conflict between man and nature and the series was firmly committed to conservation measures.

As the series grew in reputation and authority, it began to acquire a new breed of cameramen. *Survival* needed experts all over the world. City-bred film makers, no matter how skilful, were not ideal; *Survival* required men who were naturalists as well as film makers, able to work all hours of day and night, and at home in the wildest parts of the world.

One of the first was Alan Root, who made a landmark programme in 1967 when he travelled to the Galapagos, the group of islands in the Pacific, off Ecuador, where Charles Darwin found the clues to his theory of evolution. There the wildlife is unafraid of man because it has never had cause to fear him. Root filmed the giant tortoises, iguanas, boobies and gannets – and his wife, Joan, swimming among sea lions. *The Enchanted Isles*, with an introduction and commentary by the Duke of Edinburgh, who had visited the Galapagos three years earlier, was the first British natural history programme to be networked on American television.

Another acquisition was Australian Des Bartlett, the doyen of wildlife cameramen, who had filmed all Armand and Michaela Denis's *On Safari* programmes in the Fifties. Home for Des and Jen Bartlett was their Land Rover. Perhaps the most famous of the Bartlett programmes was one in which he and Jen tracked the migration of snowgeese from their nesting place on the tundra west of Hudson Bay in the Arctic to Texas and the Mississippi delta 2,500 miles south.

The *Survival* team has since grown steadily and includes several adventurous women – among them Buxton's daughter, Lucinda, whose first assignment was to film flamingoes in Kenya. She made world headlines in 1982 when she and her assistant, Annie Price, were trapped on South Georgia in the South Atlantic when Argentine troops invaded while they were filming.

Several of the 'front-liners', as they are called, pilot their own aircraft to reach remote places. Mostly, however, the travelling is in specially fitted out Land Rovers carrying equipment that includes image intensifiers to make night time filming possible, and 'cool' floodlights which will illuminate insects brilliantly without cooking them.

Survival camera crews know discomforts and dangers of all kinds. To film beavers underwater in Wyoming, Des Bartlett had to smash ice on a lake before he could enter it, and even though he wore a wet suit had to be revived by vigorous massaging from his wife after each dip. Des and Jen Bartlett came close to drowning in the Amazon when their rubber boat was damaged and

they were washed half a mile down river. John Buxton, Aubrey's cousin, was nearly trampled by buffalo in northern Canada. Dieter Plage, a mercurial West German, was attacked by a crocodile which bit through his camera mounting, and run over by an enraged tusker in Sri Lanka.

When Cindy Buxton suffered from a tooth abscess in Kenya she was days away from any dentist and had to deliver herself into the hands of an Asian with a pair of forceps. In the absence of anaesthetic, an African sat on her stomach and grasped her head and, after a 20-minute struggle, the tooth was extracted.

Tragically, there have been deaths. Lee Lyon, a young Californian trained by Plage, was covering a round-up of elephant calves in Rwanda in 1975, making her first film entirely on her own, when one of them, weighing about three-quarters of a ton, suddenly charged and trampled her. John Pearson was accidentally shot and killed on a camp site in Tanzania by a guard who, after hearing a noise, opened fire from within his tent.

Few members of the public knew or cared about the world's endangered species when

Cindy Buxton on safari in Zambia while making a Survival *programme about elephants.*

Alan Root captures a deadly black-necked cobra to film it spitting venom for Survival.

57

Survival began. The programmes, seen around the world, have been influential in awakening the public conscience.

Roving Explorer

While the Anglia Television series employs highly talented cameramen and women, the BBC has the most respected presenter of wildlife programmes in Sir David Attenborough, younger brother of movie-maker Sir Richard. Fronting innumerable series, he has done more than any other individual to popularise natural history. His *Life on Earth* in 1979 took more than three years to prepare, and was an enormous undertaking, tracing the development of living species on Earth, including man. Attenborough and his team from the BBC Natural History Unit in Bristol travelled a million and a half miles to more than 30 countries, shooting one and a quarter million feet of film, and compressing more than 3,000 million years of evolution into 13 hours of TV. Attenborough has said: 'When I was explaining the series I found it difficult to convince people. I'd say, "The first programme is an hour long and it's about worms . . ." and I could see their eyes glazing over. I knew these worms were beautiful and fascinating, but it came as a surprise to the viewer.'

In one episode he went diving off Hawaii to get a close look at humpback whales, and in the final programme he disported himself with gorillas and disappeared completely beneath a pile of black fur. Some viewers were alarmed for his safety but Attenborough said he was unconcerned. The gorillas were showing friendliness and: 'It was such a huge compliment that I couldn't think of anything except how enormously flattered I was.'

Even more people around the world have seen *The Living Planet*, completed in 1984, another 13-hour series concentrating on the interdependence of flora and fauna, geology and climate, divided into a dozen episodes each dealing with one of Earth's major environments including jungles, islands, mountains and deserts, and the creatures which live in them. It took another three years and had Attenborough jet-hopping from Borneo rain forests to Arctic islands to New York City. In the first programme he was seen within one hour in the Himalayas, Iceland, Northern Ireland, Africa and Indonesia. He said:

'We felt it was ridiculous to go on making history films that managed to behave as if *homo sapiens* didn't exist. We have looked, for example, at the way the Sherpas have adapted to mountain living, and at the planet's newest environment, the city. We do talk a lot about man's destruction of the rain forests. Of course man does perfectly dreadful things to the environment. . . .'

For one episode in *The Living Planet* which dealt with jungles, he hit on the idea of starting his words to viewers from the top of a tree and descending through layers of forest life until he reached the foot. Thus it was that he found himself climbing 150 ft up a rope. 'It was jolly tiring and I was in extremis by the time I got to the top, but I had to go through with it,' he said.

Pioneers

The pioneers of television wildlife films in 1954 were Armand and Michaela Denis, who went on to make more than 100 programmes. He was a massive Belgian chemist and she was a striking British blonde more than 20 years younger, who liked to pose with leopards. They travelled throughout Africa, South America and the Far East, trekking, hiking, climbing and canoeing, with a team of three — a cameraman, an assistant and a mechanic. Although a great deal of their filming was done near Nairobi, where they lived, they also travelled to the swamps and jungle of Borneo and New Guinea, to South America, the Sahara, Australia and Indo-China.

Beneath the sea, Hans Hass, a German diver, and Lotte, his comely wife, formerly his secretary, braved sharks for an early underwater series, *Diving to Adventure*, shot in the Caribbean in 1956. However, the greatest maker of undersea programmes has been the slightly built French naval officer, Captain Jacques-Yves Cousteau, one of the wartime inventors of the aqualung.

In 1951 he bought an old American minesweeper which he converted into a research vessel, the *Calypso*, equipped with a laboratory, workshop and diving platform, and staffed by cameramen, scientists, sailors and divers. From it flowed a stream of programmes including *The Undersea World of Jacques Cousteau* which won many awards from 1968. Dedicated to fighting pollution of the sea, Cousteau said of his films: 'I show the treasures we may lose — because if we learn to love the sea and all the creatures in it, maybe we will be clever enough to save it.'

Animal Stars

The stars of nature documentaries are, of course, animals in the wild, but trained animals also star on television, particularly in American drama series for children. The most famous of them was *Lassie*, the collie whose TV career began in 1954, 11 years after the first *Lassie* film. By 1960 she had brought 152 villains to justice, rescued 73 assorted animals and birds, and leapt through 47 windows, off 13 cliffs and on to 17 moving vehicles. She travelled 40,000 miles a year from her air-conditioned kennel on the Hollywood estate of her trainer, Rudd Weatherwax, ate the best of food and was insured for $100,000. On the set Lassie rested on a four-wheeled bed between takes.

Actually, two different animals had played the role by 1960 and the number rose to seven — including one male — over the 18 years during which 186 television programmes and movies were made, some of the films being compiled from television programmes. Lassie's fictional masters had changed almost as frequently. Her first owner on television was 11-year-old Jeff Miller (Tommy Rettig) who inherited her after the death of a neighbour; but when he moved from a farm to live in a city Lassie was taken over by seven-year-old Timmy Martin (Jon Provost) who had been rescued by Lassie after running away from an orphanage. In 1964 Lassie became the property of Corey Stuart, a forest ranger (Robert Bray), but after 1971 no longer had a permanent master and roamed the country helping people in trouble.

Fury, which began in 1955 and continued for 11 years, was the story of a black stallion presented to orphan Jim Newton by the rancher who became his new foster father. In the story, only the boy could ride the newly captured stallion, although — such are

the ways of Hollywood — 12-year-old Bobby Diamond, who played Jim, could not ride at all before getting the job.

The most unusual animal star was *Flipper*, a bottle-nosed dolphin, who made her TV debut in 1964 after a film, and had adventures with two boys, Sandy and Bud Ricks (Luke Halpin and Tommy Norden), the sons of a Florida marina ranger. The producer studied more than 80 dolphins before choosing Flipper — then known as Susie — because of her winning personality and freedom from scars. The real Flipper and her mother had been separated from Flipper's father when they were captured in Biscayne Bay for exhibition in a Miami 'seaquarium'. Then the mother died. Ricou Browning, her trainer, said:

'At the time her mother died she was still on a milk diet, and had never eaten or even tasted a live fish. Normally when this occurs the baby dolphin will die soon after its mother, but fortunately Flipper quickly learned to eat cut fish — imported Iceland herring, blue runner and mackerel.'

She was ready to perform after three months and was first ridden by Luke Halpin. He said: 'We knew Flipper would retrieve anything thrown into the water so Ricou picked me up and threw me in, signalling to Flipper to bring me back. She tried to move me every way she could without hurting me. She tried to get under me and push with her head or to take my hand in her mouth and pull, but she would never hold me tight enough for her needle-sharp teeth to make a mark. Finally, Ricou told me to grab hold of her dorsal fin. Immediately we were off and running. Flipper towed me all around the lagoon and enjoyed it as much as I did.'

Flipper went on to star in 88 episodes. Underwater sequences were filmed in Nassau in the Bahamas, and other scenes in Miami, the dolphin commuting by air in a box lined with foam rubber and kept moist by five gallons of salt water. She was a natural exhibitionist. Browning said: 'To amuse herself she'll never perform a trick the same way twice. When retrieving a ball, Flipper will first bring it back in her teeth, then balanced on a fin, then on her nose.' Animals can act humans off the screen anytime.

6
Real Lives
Dramatised Biographies

Faction is the name that has been given to television productions that are a combination of fact and fiction. These are programmes about real people and real events presented in the form of television drama with actors. Such programmes can be controversial because of the difficulty of knowing where fact ends, and fiction – or at least, conjecture – begins. There is, of course, nothing new about dramatising historical events and people. Aeschylus, the father of Greek tragedy, did it and so did Shakespeare and so did Hollywood movies (sometimes with hilarious gaffes). Television was able to do it for years without causing concern – when it was dealing with people dead for centuries.

There were, for example, series such as *Sir Francis Drake*, about the 16th-century English admiral who fought the Spanish Armada. In a 1962 series Drake was played by Terence Morgan and Queen Elizabeth I by Jean Kent. The producers went to considerable trouble to find a suitable, seaworthy ship to double as Drake's *Golden Hind* before they located, on mudflats near Colchester, Essex, the neglected hull of a motor fishing vessel built during World War Two. It had last been used by the Society for the Propagation of the Gospel as a mission ship, and had been rigged in 16th-century style for quayside gospel meetings. The old engines were removed and a new diesel installed, new decks were laid and the ship sailed to Falmouth where a long bowsprit and six new yard arms were fitted, and new sails were machined.

However, no claims were made for the truth of the stories filmed on board. Associate producer Harry Fine said at the time: 'We have tried to re-create situations in which we think Drake might have been involved. We have set him up as an embodiment of the adventurous spirit of the Elizabethan age.' The significant words were 'might have been'.

In 1970 the BBC had one of its biggest drama successes with *The Six Wives of Henry VIII* which, in its bedroom scenes at least, depended on a writer's imagination. One programme was devoted to each of the wives, Catherine of Aragon (Annette Crosbie), Anne Boleyn (Dorothy Tutin), Jane Seymour, (Anne Stallybrass), Anne of Cleves (Elvi Hale), Catherine Howard (Angela Pleasence), and Catherine Parr (Rosalie Crutchley), but the series was dominated by the figure of Henry. Australian-born, 40-year-old Keith Michell bestrode the screen in the role, changing as the weeks passed from fit, handsome 17-year-old to 20-stone, 56-year-old tyrant. By the final episode it took two dressers to help him into the padding and costume, and he spent up to four hours in the make-up department. Michell said: 'I think people like Henry because he was so very human, with weaknesses, yet also a

Getting fatter: Keith Michell midway through the series, The Six Wives of Henry VIII.

60

great glamour – rather like an American cigar-chewing impresario today. All his women expected too much of him and perhaps he expected too much of them.'

Costumes were made from specially dyed materials, while for jewellery and chains of gold the BBC bought £50 worth of junk which craftsmen hammered into shape. They were all exhibited later at the Victoria and Albert Museum.

Producer Mark Shivas says of the series, which has been seen in 78 countries: 'I suppose it has been successful because it exemplifies those things which the outside world always associates with the English – royalty and tradition. Plus, there is a bit of sex and violence in between.'

In *Elizabeth R*, which followed a year later, Glenda Jackson outdid Michell by ageing from 17 to 69 (roughly equivalent to 100 today) during the six episodes. To reproduce the Queen's baldness she could have worn a wig but Jackson bravely insisted on having her head shaved at the

Lee Remick as Jennie, Lady Randolph Churchill, *on location in Hertfordshire.*

front, and by the last episode her appearance was grotesque, for she was given a chalk-white face like a clown's. Historians said this was correct because bathing was unfashionable in 1603 and Elizabeth's make-up was permanent.

Nineteenth-century Figures

By 1975 television was moving into series about the more recent dead, who might have close relatives still living, and there was an increased concern about accuracy. *Jennie, Lady Randolph Churchill* was the life story of Sir Winston Churchill's American mother, born Jennie Jerome in 1854, who was brought to England by her mother to be launched into British society at the age of 19 and, being a lively New Yorker, dazzled society in the stuffy atmosphere of the great houses of England. Within weeks she met the 23-year-old Lord Randolph Churchill, son of the Duke of Marlborough and accepted his proposal of marriage.

Lee Remick, like Jennie, brought up in New York, but living in London, had read a biography of Jennie. 'I thought what a marvellous lady she would be to play, a one-off who wasn't following anybody's previous pattern of life . . . a woman of tremendous energy and vitality, not likely to be told what to do by anyone.' She took the idea to a producer and the part was hers.

In the same year came *Edward the Seventh*, the life story of Queen Victoria's heir, with Timothy West as Edward, Annette Crosbie as Victoria, and Robert Hardy as Prince Albert.

Executive producer Cecil Clarke was refreshingly frank about the difficulties of reconciling facts and entertainment: 'You have to set your sights at complete authenticity in all your pre-production preparation and thinking. You then have to decide whether complete authenticity is going to work dramatically and make an interesting programme, or to what degree you are going to have to bend it to make it work. If we had done *Edward the Seventh* with absolute 100 per cent authenticity it would probably have ended up a rather dull programme, an historical document rather than a viewable series. We decided to do it as a programme the public would want to see week after week and not make it simply a 13-part history lesson.'

However, departures from 100 per cent authenticity could not have been too glaring as the Queen read the script at an early stage and, on the strength of it, granted permission for filming in royal locations.

A cameo role in the series had been that of Lillie Langtry, the king's mistress, played by Francesca Annis. In *Lillie* (1978) Annis went on to play the same role through 13 episodes. The woman known as the Jersey Lily, because she was born in Jersey in the Channel Islands, was 23, and Edward the 36-year-old Prince of Wales when their affair began. Although he had a string of mistresses, she was the first acknowledged one, the first to be publicly displayed. She became an early pin-up, advertising Pears' soap, and after the affair ended she enjoyed a successful stage career.

Annis said after the filming: 'I've grown fond of Lillie, although she was far from perfect. She was selfish and used people all her life to get the success she had in her sights from childhood. She was insensitive. She wanted more than anything to be rich and famous. Lillie was tremendously healthy. She could drink all night and be up at six to go riding. At 46 she married a man 20 years younger than herself.'

Lillie provided yet another challenge for make-up artists. Annis was required to age from 16 (with her 23-inch waist corseted to 20 inches) to 70 (with plastic jowls, and bags under her eyes). The cast also included Denis Lill as the King, Anton Rodgers as her husband, Edward Langtry, Peter Egan as Oscar Wilde and Derek Smith as the sex-crazed King Leopold of the Belgians.

Prince Charles was reported to have described it as 'like watching royal home movies', and Earl Mountbatten (whose father, Prince Louis of Battenberg, Edward's nephew, was revealed in the series as being the father of Lillie's daughter Jean Marie) had his butler record episodes for him if he had to be away from home when they were transmitted.

Writer David Butler, who had also worked on *Edward the Seventh*, said: 'People remain absolutely fascinated by anything connected with royalty. One of the most remarkable events the series produced was a public acknowledgement by Earl Mountbatten about his father's relationship with Lillie. In the Victorian and Edwardian periods royals never acknowledged anything, but we wanted to make everything as accurate as possible in *Lillie* and we got permission to use this part of the story. The daughter of the romance, Jean Marie, was very bitter against Lillie for not telling her the real identity of her father, but her own daughter, Mary Malcolm, had no objection.'

At a hotel in Bournemouth where Lillie and Edward dallied, honeymoon couples asked for the room they occupied, and at a cemetery in Chester families posed for pictures beside the grave of Lillie's husband, who died mad. Letters by Lillie found in a Jersey attic were auctioned for £8,000.

Twentieth-century Sensations

Royal stories were obviously enormously popular and television was emboldened to pursue them into the 20th century in 1978 with *Edward and Mrs Simpson*, a six-part account of events leading up to the abdication of Edward the Eighth. Edward Fox was seen as the King, Cynthia Harris as Mrs Simpson, Marius Goring as George the Fifth, Dame Peggy Ashcroft as Queen Mary, and Andrew Ray as the Duke of York (later George the Sixth).

It told the couple's story from 1928, two years before their first meeting, to 1936 when the King told the nation on the radio: 'I have found it impossible to carry the heavy burden of responsibility and to discharge my duties as King as I would wish to do, without the help and support of the woman I love.'

The scandal was within the memory of many viewers, among whom opinions of the couple differed. Producer Andrew Brown

Francesca Annis as Lillie *(left) at the wedding of her brother, played by Anthony Head.*

said: 'It was vital that we presented the story as accurately as possible. We could not stray from the truth or distort it. Every aspect of the scripts was scrupulously researched, and essentially *Edward and Mrs Simpson* was a dramatic re-creation of the facts as we know them.'

It was, however, made without the blessing of the octogenarian Duchess of Windsor, the former Wallis Simpson, though it could be argued that this was reasonable since she and the ex-King had published books and articles many years earlier giving their versions of the story. However, her lawyer, Suzanne Blum, condemned the scripts as 'vulgar, platitudinous, utterly inelegant and basely commercial' and declared: 'Their Mrs Simpson bears no resemblance to the woman I have known for 40 years'.

This showed that, no matter how accurate the facts, there are always questions of interpretation in faction. American actress Cynthia Harris made Mrs Simpson a believable character but was her portrayal too harsh or too sympathetic? People who knew her might differ in their views. Cynthia Harris said at the time: 'Wallis Simpson, as I portray her, does love the King. In her words he was "the most glamorous of men in the most glamorous of worlds". She said that she couldn't believe that this man could have been so attracted to her; she knew she wasn't a beauty.'

Edward Fox, playing the King, was also aware of the problems: 'I thought it would be very interesting to do, but very difficult. I said to the producer, "You can't get it right, but you mustn't get it wrong." The scenes I found the hardest to play are those where you cannot find documented evidence. The constitutional crisis was much the easiest because on the government side you can draw from the words said. There are masses of documents. With the private life, either with Mrs Simpson or with anybody else, you can only get a flavour. Presumably there will be people who will say "It was not like that", and they will be right. So long as the spirit is caught, that is all you can do.'

Millions around the world will always see the face and mannerisms of Fox when the name of Edward the Eighth is mentioned, although Fox declared: 'I'm not at all like Edward VIII. Nothing like him. He was a *wildly* glamorous figure, *immensely* glamorous.'

The Kennedy Story

Andrew Brown went on to produce *Kennedy*, the story of JFK from the beginning of his presidential campaign in 1960 to his death in Dallas on 22 November 1963. (It was first shown on the 20th anniversary of that day in 1983.) The surprising aspect was that it was made by a British company, although it used American actors: Martin Sheen as John F. Kennedy, John Shea as Robert, E. G. Marshall as Joseph, Blair Brown as Jacqueline, and Vincent Gardenia as J. Edgar Hoover, the FBI chief, determined to discover the Kennedys in sexual indiscretions. Possibly the American networks were too close to the events to make such a series themselves, but they screened it and received it warmly; *Kennedy* was the first British mini-series to be networked in the USA.

What decided an English company to go to America and make the series? Director Jim Goddard said: 'Americans underestimate Kennedy's impact on the rest of the world. They are always surprised to hear that people were crying in the streets of England when they heard the news of his death. Kennedy was a world figure. We have every right to make this series and we can bring a much-needed objectivity to it.'

Writer Reg Gadney spent two and a half years researching and writing, and was required to provide at least two different sources for every fact, though the Kennedy family was not approached for help. Gadney said he was offered the opportunity to meet Jacqueline Onassis (the former First Lady) by a mutual acquaintance, but turned it down for fear it might affect his objectivity.

Producer Andrew Brown said at the time: 'We never put words into people's mouths unless we can substantiate them. We want to be fair and truthful because we only have one chance of doing this and we want to get it right. First of all, we have a duty to, and secondly, we would have a legal problem if we did not. So everything in the scripts has been checked and rechecked.'

Kennedy's womanising was one problem that exercised the production team. Jim

Edward the Seventh
(Timothy West)
popularised dramas
about the royal family.

Jeremy Irons and
Anthony Andrews as
Oxford undergraduates
in Brideshead Revisited.

Patrick Allen as stern crammer Thomas Gadgrind in Charles Dickens's Hard Times.

Left Captain James Onedin (Peter Gilmore) surveys his empire.

Below stairs conference between butler, maid and cook in Upstairs, Downstairs.

Goddard said: 'We would be naive to leave it out. Therefore we have dealt with it in a way which acknowledges it, but balances it against his best achievements. There is no point in deifying a politician if you want him to be acceptable to the public. Kennedy was a man with all the faults and blemishes of any real human being. So, in order to illustrate his exceptional gifts, you have to show all the things he overcame to be better than everyone else at what he did.'

Settings such as the Oval Office in the White House had to be re-created for the series. On Pier 62 by New York's Hudson River an enormous warehouse, normally used as a long-stay car park, was converted into White House rooms with everything in them as they were in JFK's day, including his rocking chair and the model of PT 109, the torpedo boat he had commanded. Instead of filming in Dallas the team re-created the emotional day of the assassination in Richmond, Virginia, which looked more like the Dallas of 1963 than Dallas itself. The original motorcade car was a 1961 Lincoln Continental convertible, 'stretched' to give it three rows of seats. That car, the only one of

Martin Sheen as Kennedy *and Blair Brown as Jackie re-enact the fatal motorcade.*

its kind, was in Ford's museum in Michigan, but the team made a replica by cutting a 1961 Lincoln in half, and joining parts from four other Lincolns which they cannibalised.

With the co-operation of the police, the main street was cordoned off for six blocks and the traffic flow reversed for the filming of the motorcade sequence. Because of fears that a madman might attempt to kill the television JFK, a police helicopter hovered overhead and plain clothes police were present in force, some on rooftops and others mingling with the 1,000 extras brought in for crowd scenes and surreptitiously searched by wardrobe assistants who kitted them out. Six first-aid stations were set up.

Re-examination of a Hero

Kennedy did no harm to the memory of the 35th President, but *The Last Place on Earth* in 1985 brought about a re-examination of the legend of Captain Scott's doomed expedition to the South Pole. At the end of the first decade of this century Antarctica was the one major territory unexplored, and two men were obsessed with the ambition to be first to reach the South Pole. They were Norway's Roald Amundsen and England's Capt. Robert Falcon Scott. Scott lost the race but achieved national hero status after dying bravely 11 miles short of his base camp on the journey home in 1912.

The series was filmed in Canada, Norway and Greenland under taxing conditions. Everything required, including horses, had to be flown in, and it was so cold that lubricating oil in the film cameras had to be drained and replaced by graphite to keep them rolling. Producer Tim van Rellim said:

'At any one time a crew numbering as many as 100 and a cast ranging between 20 and 50 were assembled, shivering, on the permafrost for 10 hours at a stretch. I don't think any one of us, neither crew nor cast, quite understood what it would be like to work in freezing conditions day after day, sometimes starting at 5.30 in the morning six days a week. We knew we were going to places where it would be pretty tough. After all, we were looking to re-create some of the awful conditions encountered by Scott and Amundsen, but none of us really knew how bad it would be.'

The script by Trevor Griffiths took a cool look at Scott. Amundsen (played by Sverre Anker Ousdal) was seen as a professional, Scott (Martin Shaw) as an amateur, arrogant and obstinate. Sir Peter Scott, the explorer's son, and Lord Kennet, son of the explorer's widow, made it known that they were unhappy about the series, but director Ferdinand Fairfax (who had earlier made another faction, *Churchill: the Wilderness Years*, starring Robert Hardy as Churchill before World War Two) said: 'It's fair that the myth should be looked at again. I'm not setting out to upset Scott's family but descendants of famous people have to realise that it's legitimate to look at the behaviour and achievements of their forebears. Nobody's sacred.'

That is now an accepted creed in television, and history may be moving out of the hands of historians and into those of television writers and producers, with millions throughout the world getting their only insight into people and events from TV series which, if they are to win mass audiences, must above all be entertaining.

Captain Scott's team trek across the frozen wastes of Antarctica in The Last Place on Earth.

7

Best of British

Drama Productions

The impact of *The Forsyte Saga* was immense. In Britain, in 1967, church services were curtailed to allow congregations to get home to watch John Galsworthy's story of a family of London merchants from the 1870s to 1920s, as it unfolded over 26 weeks. It brought personal triumphs for Eric Porter as the unsympathetic lawyer, Soames Forsyte, and New Zealand actress Nyree Dawn Porter (no relation) as his cool, beautiful first wife, Irene. A scene in which he raped her, though handled most discreetly, was considered daring at the time.

The *Saga* went on to make a big impact in America in 1969, although no concessions had been made to a transatlantic audience, and it was shown on National Educational Television rather than a major network. 'The greatest soap opera ever filmed,' declared *Time*. Two years later one US station showed the *Saga* non-stop over 23 hours and 50 minutes, the longest scheduled fiction programmes on record. In 1970 Russia became the 45th country to buy it, and the total viewing figures reached 160 million.

Eric Porter said: 'The *Saga* sold round the world and Soames spotters were everywhere. They buttonholed me in Detroit, in Malta and a Spanish beach. There was no hiding place; even in Budapest this large lady with dyed hair came beaming over, placed a plump hand on my chest and said, "Aaaach, Soooames Forsyte".' Nyree Dawn Porter received proposals of marriage from far-off countries, and Susan Hampshire, who played

Fleur, Soames's daughter by a second marriage, reported that in Norway a crowd of 60,000 gathered to see her – in a town of only 10,000.

An even more significant result of the *Saga*'s success was that America's Public Service Television – a chain of nearly 300 stations – launched a *Masterpiece Theatre* series of British programmes, introduced at peak time on Sunday nights by Alistair Cooke. It began in 1971 with *The First Churchills*, about the family of the first Duke of Marlborough, which was written and produced by Donald Wilson, *The Forsyte Saga*'s producer, and co-starred Susan Hampshire with John Neville.

The Forsyte Saga no longer rates among the BBC's best-sellers, largely because it was made in black and white, the last major series lacking colour, but it gave the BBC a big breakthrough in foreign sales, particularly of dramas adapted from great novels. The *Saga*'s sales were, in fact, overtaken by another 26-part series starring Susan Hampshire, *The Pallisers*, made in 1974. It was known at the BBC as 'the 26 Trollopes' because it was based on Anthony Trollope's account of a Victorian arranged marriage, between the flighty Lady Glencora (Hampshire) and a high-principled politician, Plantaganet Palliser (Philip Latham).

Eric Porter rejoined *Forsyte* producer Donald Wilson in 1978 when he made *Anna Karenina*, Leo Tolstoy's story of infidelity and tragedy in 19th-century Russia, with

68

Nicola Pagett as Anna Karenina; *Eric Porter as her boring husband.*

Nicola Pagett in the role for which Greta Garbo was celebrated, as Anna, a government official's wife who became pregnant by a rakish officer, Count Vronsky (Stuart Wilson). Porter played her dull husband Karenin, complaining: 'Soames was a frozen twit; Karenin is another. I seem to have cornered the market in po-faced characters. It's my face, you know; with my face you can't play cheerful, cheeky, jolly roles.'

Anna followed Tolstoy's *War and Peace*, the epic story about the Russian role in the Napoleonic wars, made in 20 episodes lasting 15 hours, with 200 speaking parts and 1,000 Yugoslav soldiers deployed in the battle scenes and the retreat from Moscow. Morag Hood, only 5 ft tall, was chosen from 1,000 applicants to play Natasha Rostova from teenage to middle age, co-starring with Anthony Hopkins as rich Pierre Bezuhof, whom Natasha married.

Charles Dickens has also been well served by British television. A 1975 version of

Every inch the prosperous merchant: Eric Porter as Soames in The Forsyte Saga.

David Copperfield, with David Yelland as the hero, Arthur Lowe as Micawber, and Martin Jarvis as Uriah Heep, has been seen in 63 countries, though Granada's *Hard Times*, made two years later, has been seen in 82, achieving the widest circulation of any British TV adaptation of a novel.

For *Hard Times*, Dickens's protest against educators, which starred Patrick Allen as Thomas Gradgrind, cramming facts into his children, Louisa and Thomas, Granada built a vast location set covering five acres of a former railway goods yard in Manchester. Fifty men built on it a full-scale circus 'big top', a Victorian version of a Ferris wheel, swingboats, roundabouts, sideshow booths and 12 caravans; and the scenes played there involved 300 performers, including tumblers, bareback riders and boxers, plus 15 horses and a dancing bear. Another location was a valley in the Anglezarke Moors, 20 miles from Manchester, where a mine shaft was sunk, and wooden huts erected for make-up, wardrobe and catering services. Horses and carriages were transported there, and coaches ferried crew and actors.

Modern Novelists

Among drama serials based on the work of modern novelists, *Poldark* in 1976 was an adaptation of Winston Graham's novels about an 18th-century Cornish squire. Dashing Ross Poldark (Robin Ellis) returned unexpectedly to Cornwall from fighting the Americans in the War of Independence to find he was believed killed. His father was dead, the family home in disrepair, its copper mines idle, and the girl he planned to marry engaged to his cousin. The serial involved smuggling, famine and rebellion.

Brideshead Revisited dramatised Evelyn Waugh's story about an Oxford undergraduate whose life became dominated by his friendship with a wealthy Catholic family. Waugh, writing during World War Two, described it as: 'A very beautiful book, to bring tears, about the very rich, beautiful, high-born people who live in palaces and have no troubles except what they make themselves, and these are mainly the demons of sex and drink which, after all, are easy to bear as troubles go nowadays.'

As a young reporter on the Brighton *Evening Argus* Derek Granger had once interviewed Waugh, convalescing at a hotel; 25 years later, as a drama producer at Granada, Granger took on the job of turning *Brideshead* into a serial. About one and a half hours out of a projected 13 had been completed when all ITV productions were halted by a strike. The strike lasted 10 weeks and by the time work restarted contracts covering artists and locations had expired and needed renegotiating, while some of the cast were no longer available. It would be costly to go on, but it would be costly to scrap the production. Granger was told to go on.

The cost rose to £5 million, which was considerably more than originally planned, and at one time *Brideshead* was regarded as in danger of becoming a television equivalent of the film industry's ill-fated *Caesar and Cleopatra*. In fact, it was an enormous success, slow moving but majestic and beautifully photographed.

The story was told by Charles Ryder (Jeremy Irons), an army captain posted in World War Two to Brideshead Castle, Wiltshire home of the eccentric Marchmain family. (The building seen in the serial was Castle Howard, Yorkshire seat of the then BBC chairman, George Howard.) Flashbacks recalled Ryder's first meeting with the pampered Marchmain son, Sebastian (Anthony Andrews), and his posturing cronies at Oxford. Over the years Ryder, a painter, was then embroiled with the family in Venice and Africa, on transatlantic liners and in London salons as Sebastian, who never travelled without his teddy bear, degenerated into alcoholism. There were cameos from Sir Laurence Olivier as Lord Marchmain, Claire Bloom as his wife, and Sir John Gielgud as Ryder's father. 'The nearest thing to perfection that the TV serial has managed in its entire history,' wrote one critic when it was screened in 1981.

Four years later the BBC spent even more to make *Tender Is the Night* from F. Scott Fitzgerald's novel of love and madness, about rich Americans in search of fun and games in Europe after World War One. Peter Strauss played Dick Diver, a young American psychiatrist who thought he could mix therapy and love by marrying schizophrenic Nicole Warren (Mary Steenburgen), resulting in scenes that mirrored episodes in Fitzgerald's own marriage. Filmed in the south of France and Switzerland, it was set in the frivolous jazz age of the Twenties, and scriptwriter Dennis Potter employed the same technique he used in *Pennies from Heaven* and laced events with songs such as *I'm Forever Blowing Bubbles* and *Poor Butterfly*. But it was not as successful as *Brideshead*.

Indian Sagas

Two major drama productions of 1984 were set in India, and following the film *Gandhi* helped promote a worldwide fascination with India and boost its tourism. *The Far Pavilions*, from a book by M. M. Kaye, was a lavish mini-series set in Victorian days. Its most spectacular scene was a mile-long caravan of people and animals – a thousand extras, 20 elephants, 120 bullocks, plus goats, sheep and cows. This represented the

procession of two Indian princesses, Anjuli (Amy Irving) and her spoilt, petulant half-sister Shushila (Sneh Gupta) travelling to arranged marriages, with an escort of soldiers from the elite Corps of Guides commanded by a British officer (Ben Cross) who had been Anjuli's childhood sweetheart.

It was a Hollywood-style extravaganza but suffered from inevitable comparisons with *The Jewel in the Crown*, drawn from the four Paul Scott novels known as the Raj Quartet.

The story was about love-hate relationships between Indians and Britons in the turbulent last years of British rule between 1942 and 1947. Susan Wooldridge played Daphne Manners, a gawky, gauche English nurse, whose rape in a public garden set in train far-reaching events. Art Malik played

Demelza (Angharad Rees) and Ross (Robin Ellis) with ore from a family mine in Poldark.

Hari Kumar, a young Indian accused of the rape; he had been educated at an English public school but in India he could not speak his native tongue and was accepted neither by the Indians nor the ruling British. Tim Pigott-Smith played Ronald Merrick, a sneering, less educated police superintendent who arrested him, and later became an army major. The story involved class and education, religion and social responsibilities, loyalty and cruelty.

Four months were spent filming in India. Granada shipped out 300 containers ranging from a three-ton generator to a suitcase full of aerosol sprays, and from a mobile kitchen to six portable lavatories. Unexpected

71

problems arose daily. A scene at a temple required beggars as extras, and a suitable group found on a street corner agreed to be collected by coach and taken to a temple for filming. Then they changed their minds; a rumour had started that the filming was a blind and they were to be transported to a hospital and sterilised by vasectomy. In the end they went to the temple and tried hard to persuade the actors entering and leaving to part with real money each time.

Temperatures ranged from over 100°F in Mysore, where the company drank 200 gallons of soft drinks in one day, to freezing in snow a month later in Simla, where Dame Peggy Ashcroft, playing a former missionary, and Rachel Kempson, playing Lady Manners, the nurse's aunt, huddled in a bed with hot water bottles to try to keep warm between takes.

Filming was completed in England, with the Bibighar gardens, scene of the rape, recreated in a Lancashire quarry, and an Indian railway platform on a disused station in Buckinghamshire, with 130 Indians and people of Indian descent from Luton, Watford, Oxford and Aylesbury as passengers; many of them had to be shown how to wear dhotis.

The spectacular wedding procession for two Indian princesses in The Far Pavilions.

Short Stories

Tales of the Unexpected, an anthology of short stories featuring a twist in the tail, which has been seen in more than 100 countries, began with stories by Roald Dahl. Anglia Television's Sir John Woolf met the writer for the first time at a Christmas party and when Dahl asked, 'How would you like to make a television series of my stories?' Sir John grabbed the opportunity. They began in 1979, mixing suspense, horror and black comedy. International stars were signed, among them Joseph Cotten, José Ferrer, Sir John Gielgud, Derek Jacobi, Sir John Mills, Timothy West, Susan George, Wendy Hiller and Joan Collins.

When all the suitable Dahl stories had been used up, more stories of a similar nature were bought or commissioned from other writers, and over 100 programmes have been made, some of them small gems, others meretricious. Many viewers were intrigued by the opening titles in which a silhouette of a sinuous dancer was seen undulating. The dancer was Karen Standley, a Buckinghamshire secretary, who said:

'I had to wear a white bodystocking and white tights with white greasepaint all over my arms, face and neck. It kept melting under the hot studio lights while I danced to the music. It was horrible and very uncomfortable and it took three baths to wash it all off.'

Incidentally, an American series, *Alfred Hitchcock Presents*, which began in 1955, also featured stories of mystery and suspense with surprise endings. Hitchcock directed fewer than a score of the 260 himself, though he picked the stories, read the scripts and introduced the programmes. One of the most memorable was *Lamb to the Slaughter* in which Barbara Bel Geddes played a police chief's wife who battered him to death with a frozen leg of lamb, which she then served to be eaten by the investigating detectives. The story was by Roald Dahl.

From the Stage

Television also adapts plays from the stage, and from 1976 in *Laurence Olivier Presents* Britain's greatest actor presented his own productions of 20th-century plays, each of which he had chosen as the best of its year. Olivier himself appeared in *The Collection* by Harold Pinter (representing 1960), and his wife, Joan Plowright, starred in James Bridie's *Daphne Laureola* (1949). Other plays were *Hindle Wakes* (1912), *Come Back, Little Sheba* (1950), *Cat on a Hot Tin Roof* (1955) and *Saturday, Sunday, Monday* (1973). They were seen in 89 countries.

However, the most ambitious series of adaptations from the stage was that in which over six years from 1978 the BBC filmed the complete works of William Shakespeare – 37 plays including even little performed works such as *Timon of Athens*, *Titus Andronicus* and *Pericles*. The idea was to record the work of England's greatest dramatist for millions who had never seen one of his plays in their lives. Shaun Sutton, head of BBC TV drama, said: 'It's an act of faith. It had to be done and we were the people who had to do it. Eventually I think all 37 plays will be housed in school and university libraries all over the world.'

The budget was large, about a third coming from American backers. Finding them was no problem, but there was a

A man viewers loved to hate: Ronald Merrick (Tim Pigott-Smith) in The Jewel in the Crown.

backlash in the American television industry. Unions and independent programme makers were jealous of Britain's highly visible presence on the Public Broadcasting Service, which they had referred to derisively for years as the Principally British Service. (The reason for the British programmes is that America has rarely made classic drama of the kind at which Britain excels.) They objected to American money funding jobs in other countries and said that if American money was involved there should be jobs for some American actors. Sutton replied that he had nothing against American actors but a mixture of British and American accents would be unhappy. In fact, the BBC planned to cast black American actor James Earl Jones as Othello, but Equity, the British actors' trade union, refused to allow this, and insisted on a Briton. The role went to Anthony Hopkins.

All the plays had different casts and a number of different producers and directors worked on them. The main criticism of the first productions was that they were bland, but after a year the versatile and imaginative

Jonathan Miller took over, saying: 'People still think of Shakespeare in terms of Olivier or Gielgud. Why should they? I think we should look for a little more pioneering novelty for today's audience. It's a bit disappointing to see a repetition of the orthodox.'

His first production was *The Taming of the Shrew* with lanky comic John Cleese as Petruchio. He also cast Cockney Bob Hoskins as Iago in *Othello*. However, the most popular play worldwide has been *As You Like It*, seen in 50 countries, which was recorded at Glamis Castle in Scotland with Helen Mirren as Rosalind.

Masters and Servants

Among original dramas, written for television, a popular and influential series was *Upstairs, Downstairs*, which began in 1971, a saga of the lives of masters and servants in a London house between 1903 and 1930.

When viewers first visited 165 Eaton Place, Edward the Seventh was on the throne, and the fustiness of Victorian manners and morals was beginning to be swept away. The owner of the house was the aristocratic Lady Marjorie Bellamy (Rachel Gurney), a Prime Minister's daughter, destined to die on the *Titanic*. Her husband, Richard (David Langton), was a politician, correct and honest, but much helped by his wife's money and friends. James (Simon Williams), their amorous son, and Elizabeth (Nicola Pagett), their rebellious daughter, were the other principal members of the family.

Below stairs was a formidable hierarchy of servants watched over by Hudson, the dour Scottish butler (Gordon Jackson). The day before the first episode was recorded Jackson was in a car crash. 'I needed five stitches around an eye and my right hand was broken,' he said. 'In that first episode I did everything with my left hand and kept the undamaged profile to the camera.' Nearest to him in seniority was Mrs Bridges (Angela Baddeley), the grumpy but warm-hearted cook for whom 'Mrs' was a courtesy title; she had never been married. Baddeley claimed to have done a lot of baking herself in the studio kitchen while playing the role. 'We used to have little tea parties and I made a special chocolate cake which everybody loved.'

There were also Rose (Jean Marsh), a loyal, discreet housemaid, later lady's maid; Sarah (Pauline Collins), a pert parlourmaid; and at different times, a footman, a scullery maid and a chauffeur. The staff slept in attics and worked in the basement, covering miles every day fetching and carrying.

The idea was conceived beside a swimming pool in the south of France where actresses Jean Marsh and Eileen Atkins dreamed up a series about two mischievous maids. Marsh duly became Rose; Atkins intended to play Sarah but was in a play when production started.

The producer was John Hawkesworth, who began by scouring files of *The Times*, House of Commons debates, store and fashion catalogues, songbooks and theatre programmes in search of ideas for plot incidents and conversational points. By making Bellamy a politician, the series was able to reflect events and concerns of the era such as political scandals, the Great War, the suffragette movement, the General Strike, the Wall Street crash and the jazz craze.

Upstairs, Downstairs was more than a soap; it was a real family portrait and an evocation of an era, watched by 300 million in 50 countries. In America, where it was seen on the Public Broadcasting Service, it won five Emmy Awards, and CBS created an American version, *Beacon Hill*. This was set in the home of a Boston attorney in the 1920s; Hudson, the Scot, became Hacker, a Londoner, and Mrs Bridges became William Pipe, a male, black cook. It flopped.

Hawkesworth meanwhile had moved on to a second essay in the manners of yesteryear. *The Duchess of Duke Street*, made for the BBC in 1976, was another upstairs, downstairs saga based on Rosa Lewis, owner and hostess of the Cavendish Hotel in London's Jermyn Street, which was virtually a club for Edwardian aristocrats, officers and sportsmen. Lewis had been a skivvy at 12, but began moving up the downstairs ladder when she learned to cook. She married a butler and then bought the hotel with

Jean Marsh, one of the creators of Upstairs, Downstairs, *receives an Emmy Award for it.*

some help, it was thought, from the future Edward the Seventh. Lewis, who died in 1952 at the age of 83, became perky Louisa Trotter (played by Gemma Jones) in the series and the hotel became the Bentinck. 'The series is not a biography of Rosa,' Hawkesworth pointed out. 'Because it is fiction we can have little Louisa doing anything we want.'

Food and its preparation played an important part in the series and the credits included the name of a cookery adviser, Michael Smith, who prepared dishes in his own kitchen and then rushed them to the studios. For one scene a turbot had to be seen at six different stages of cooking, which meant buying six fish, each 23 inches long. For another he required 400 pork pies. Some – which had to be eaten – were real, or 'practical' in TV parlance. Others were filled with sawdust.

Difficult Roles

In 1977 Lord Grade was convinced that the world was ready for a television life of Christ – not in a religious slot but as star-studded, peak-time viewing. His *Jesus of Nazareth*, a co-production with Italy's RAI Television filmed in North Africa, was to be seen by more than 200 million people around the world.

Christ was played at different ages by five different actors. The first was a newly born baby, actually a girl, but director Franco Zeffirelli said: 'Who's going to peek under the blanket?' Others were aged two, five and twelve, with Robert Powell as the mature Jesus in what seemed to many to be a definitive performance. His eyes were mesmeric, but Powell said:

'Christ was the most difficult of roles. At one time I had a couple of days off and I thought I'd fly back to London for a breather but I was afraid I'd lose my grasp on the part. You can't be Jesus one moment and Robert Powell shopping in the local supermarket at home the next.'

Other stars flew in and out of the locations in Morocco and Tunisia: James Mason, as Joseph of Aramathea, from Switzerland, Rod Steiger (Pontius Pilate) from Malibu, Anthony Quinn (Caiaphas) from Italy, Anne Bancroft (Mary Magdalene) from New York, Sir Ralph Richardson (Simeon) and Sir Laurence Olivier (Nicodemus) from London. As many as 1,500 costumes were needed for a day's shooting. They were dyed in pastel colours from local berries as they had been 2,000 years before. The 400 sets of armour came from Rome.

Zeffirelli changed many familiar images. 'Traditionally you see Jesus sitting at a long table for the Last Supper,' he said. 'This is totally false. Perhaps painters needed this arrangement so they could show each disciple's face, but in fact people sat around on straw mats and ate off a central mat.' Nor was Christ seen carrying the entire cross, which Zeffirelli was advised was an impossible feat, but the crosspiece or parible; that alone weighed at least 80 lb.

While the story of Christ is a timeless one, television has also made dramas about highly topical subjects, and a series in 1987 dealt with one that was unknown and unforeseen even a few years earlier. *Intimate Contact* concerned a man dying of Aids. In the first drama on the subject to be made in Britain, Daniel Massey boldly essayed the role of Clive Gregory, a senior executive of an electronics company, with a wife (Claire Bloom) and two teenage children. After he collapsed on a golf course it was discovered that he had Aids, which he had contracted from a prostitute, following a party to celebrate a big contract. The discovery led to ostracism. Massey said:

'Aids is already changing the way we live. We cannot turn a blind eye to it any longer. It wasn't really until the media took it up that anything was done at all. Until now Aids has been very much linked with the homosexual community – an area that should without question be explored. But there is a lot of complacency among heterosexuals – particularly young people – that it couldn't happen to them. That misconception has now been blown apart.'

8
Hollywood Tales
American Dramas

'As American as home-baked apple pie,' said its fans. 'As gooey as molasses,' said its critics. *The Waltons* was a folksy phenomenon, a strangely old-fashioned serial for the Seventies about a sawmill-operating family in the Blue Ridge mountains of Virginia during the depression of the Thirties, but it ran to 220 episodes over nine years from 1972. It was based on a novel by Virginian-born Earl Hamner Jr, which had already yielded a 1963 film (*Spencer's Mountain* with Henry Fonda) and a sentimental Christmas TV movie in 1971, *The Homecoming*.

The family was a devoted one. The hero was the oldest of seven children, a teenager, John-Boy, played by Richard Thomas (representing Hamner as a youth). His father, John, who was strong, was played by Ralph Waite; his mother, Olivia, who was loving, by Michael Learned. There were grandparents who were venerated, and a dog named Reckless who was cherished. The stories extolled honesty, thrift, chastity and family unity. Hamner (later creator and co-executive producer of *Falcon Crest*) had no doubts about why it was such a success:

'All over the world family life is under attack. We provide a reminder of those vanishing values. By showing how one family sustained itself during those dark days I hope we have been reassuring and given the audience some sort of strength at a time when an economic depression is threatening to return.'

At breakfast in The Waltons: *Michael Learned as Olivia and Ralph Waite as John.*

Little House on the Prairie, which began in 1974, had similar unpretentious characters and a similar emphasis on traditional values, though it was set in the 1870s. Based on novels by Laura Ingalls Wilder, it related the struggles of the pioneering Ingalls family, homesteaders surviving on the plains of Plumb Creek, Minnesota. The family consisted of Charles Ingalls (played by Michael Landon, the ex-*Bonanza* star, who was also the producer), his wife, Caroline (Karen

77

Grassle), their children, Laura, Mary and Carrie, and a dog, Jack.

An America of a very different kind was depicted in *Washington Behind Closed Doors* in 1977, for this was set in the world of modern wheeler-dealing politics and power ploys, and honesty did not figure largely. It was a fictionalised account of the Watergate scandal, which began in 1972 with the arrest of five men attempting to bug the offices of the Democratic National Committee in Washington, and culminated in the downfall of President Richard Nixon. It was based on *The Company*, a novel by John Erlichman, one of Nixon's aides jailed after Watergate, who watched it in a federal prison camp in Arizona where he was inmate 7994, and approved. 'It's sensational,' was his verdict. 'It captures the essence of Washington politics beautifully.'

In the serial the break-in took place in California instead of Washington, and a prologue declared that all the events and characters were fictional, but no one was deceived. The sinister President Richard Monckton was clearly based on Nixon, though Jason Robards, who played him, said he had not consciously imitated the disgraced President. However, Robards was not a Nixon admirer:

'Every time Nixon came on TV I used to think, "Here comes old Tricky Dicky with the usual load of lies", and I just couldn't stand it. I couldn't believe it when he ran for President in the first place. Everybody said what a rotter he was for years but nobody did a hatchet job on him until Watergate. Nixon gave me the creeps, so maybe he got into my subsconscious. At the time I thought I got it all from the script.'

Other characters were also recognisable. Frank Flaherty (Robert Vaughn), the White House Chief of Staff, was modelled on H. R. Haldeman, Nixon's Chief of Staff, also jailed as a result of Watergate, retiring President Esker Anderson (Andy Griffith) on President Lyndon Johnson, and William Martin (Cliff Robertson), Director of the CIA, on Richard Helms.

War Stories

Holocaust, made in 1978, was a controversial series dealing with the Nazi extermination of Jews. It told the story of a family of Berlin Jews named Weiss (the parents played by Fritz Weaver and Rosemary Harris) from 1935 to 1945, and followed members of the family from the Warsaw ghetto to Auschwitz. Most of them died – in torture chambers, death camp ovens or mass executions by machine guns. In one scene set in Poland SS men herded Jews into a wooden synagogue and fired the building with petrol. The series was filmed in Austria and Germany, including Berlin, and mixed scripted scenes with archive newsreel footage.

Ian Holm, David Warner and Tom Bell portrayed three of the Nazi hierarchy, Heinrich Himmler, Reinhard Heydrich and Adolf Eichmann. Meryl Streep was seen as the German wife of a Jewish hero, and Michael Moriarty played Erik Dorf, a lawyer who became a sadistic SS major, but most Germans were depicted as ordinary people enmeshed in Nazism. Producer Robert Berger said:

'We tried to do something like this three years ago but the TV companies told us that it was a downer. In America now we share the tremendous resurgence of interest in the war, but we did not intend making a straight documentary; it's really four love stories about relationships in time of tremendous stress.'

The series caused controversy wherever it was shown. In Britain an 81-year-old Jewish widow killed herself after watching an episode. In America it achieved near-record viewing figures. It was also shown in West Germany, and many young Germans admitted to thinking seriously for the first time about the actions of their parents. Nevertheless, some complained that it trivialised awful events and turned a dreadful chapter of 20th-century history into soap opera. Playwright Dennis Potter wrote: 'The case against *Holocaust* is not that it is bad soap opera, but worse – much worse – that it is very good soap opera.' Others thought that it was right that a younger generation to whom talk of the war was boring should know what happened.

Shogun, in 1980, dealt with war in an earlier century and a remote land. It was adapted by James Clavell from his novel about a 17th-century British seaman, John Blackthorne, shipwrecked in Japan, and becoming a sword-wielding samurai in the service of a warlord. The role went to Richard Chamberlain (because, he said, Albert Finney and Sean Connery were unavailable). Toshiro Mifune was the warlord, and Yoko Shimada a girl for whom Blackthorne fell.

It was filmed in Japan in 100 degrees heat, scenes of a storm at sea being shot in a tank in a Tokyo studio, with aircraft engines churning the water. Chamberlain said: 'We spent months filming in Japan. The heat was killing. We had sound problems and we had language problems – you try doing a love scene with a gorgeous woman who doesn't speak English and whose wig is fast becoming unglued in the heat. At one point we were literally stuck together.'

In a world already intrigued by Japanese martial arts the serial increased the interest, and stores offered samurai swords and *Shogun*-style wall decorations.

The Winds of War concerned World War Two, and was an adaptation of Herman Wouk's novel about an American naval officer involved at the highest level in international events leading up to America's entry into the war. It spanned a period of two and a half years from mid-1939 as Hitler prepared to march into Poland, to the bombing of Pearl Harbor in December 1941.

The 16-hour serial was claimed to be the most expensive television production ever made when it was shown in 1983. It cost £25 million and involved 14 months shooting in 400 locations in six countries – Germany, Italy, Austria, Yugoslavia, Britain and the United States. The filming began in 1980 on the liner *Queen Mary* in Long Beach, California and ended back in California, where 200 sailors from the USS *Kitty Hawk* were recruited as extras in a reconstruction of the Japanese attack on Pearl Harbor on the 40th anniversary of the raid. Director Dan Curtis shot a million feet of film (equal to about 185 hours screen time) which was a year in the editing. There were 285 speaking roles and thousands of extras. Costume supervisor Tommy Welsh had to arrange clothing for 30,000 people, representing eight nations.

Robert Mitchum alone had 100 changes of costume. He starred as Commander 'Pug' Henry, a US Navy officer – a role for which, at 65, he looked too old. Henry was sent as a military attaché to a series of European capitals, and as an unofficial emissary of President Franklin D. Roosevelt (Ralph Bellamy) met all the wartime leaders, including Hitler, Stalin, Mussolini and Churchill. The serial was also about Henry's family: his restless wife, Rhoda (Polly Bergen), who fell for engineer Palmer Kirby (Peter Graves); his daughter Madeline (Lisa Eilbacher), a college student in Washington; and his sons Warren (Ben Murphy), a naval pilot in Florida, and Byron (Jan Michael Vincent) who wandered through Europe, falling in love with an American Jewish girl, Natalie Jastrow (Ali MacGraw) and becoming trapped in Poland.

In the United States it broke all records with 140 million watching at least part of it, a figure not beaten by *North and South* in 1985, although (with its sequel making up 24 episodes) the latter was claimed to have been even more costly. It dealt with the American Civil War, and coincidentally, also included Robert Mitchum in its cast.

Based on a novel by John Jakes, it was nothing less than an attempt to make a new *Gone With the Wind*, with gallant cavalry officers, evil plantation owners and Southern belles. The principals were two friends with different backgrounds and loyalties: Orry Main, a Southern gentleman (Patrick Swayze), and George Hazard (James Read), a Northerner from a family of industrialists, who met at West Point military academy but later found themselves on opposing sides.

The series followed an American trend of the time in having the chief roles played by actors little known before the series began, and supporting roles played by big stars. Mitchum was seen as an army surgeon, James Stewart as an attorney, Gene Kelly as a senator, Olivia de Havilland (who was, of course, in *Gone With the Wind*) as a nurse and Elizabeth Taylor as madame of a New Orleans brothel.

Lesley-Anne Down appeared as Madeline Fabray, a Creole beauty in love with Main – and suffered in the interests of the series. Firstly, her waist was squeezed from 28 inches to 22½. 'That makes your feet go numb,' she said. 'We were wearing those corsets for 14 hours a day. It takes several hours for the red marks to go.' Then she was outfitted with 31 substantial dresses, the heaviest weighing 45 lb. 'You've got all the weight and a wig,' she said. 'You can't scratch your head and its getting hotter by the minute.'

Birth of the Mini-series

The term 'mini-series' was coined in the mid-Seventies for American serialisations of novels, often of four or six long episodes scheduled on successive nights. These series were not particularly short by European standards, but in America conventional series commonly run weekly in seasons for as long as they are popular, which can be years.

The first mini-series, in 1975, was *Rich Man, Poor Man*, made to be shown in six episodes of 95 minutes each (though sometimes screened as 12 programmes of 50 minutes duration). It was adapted from a novel by Irwin Shaw, about two sons of an immigrant baker from the end of World War Two until the Sixties. Executive producer Harve Bennett gave credit for the idea to Britain's *Upstairs, Downstairs*. There was no obvious similarity in the stories but Bennett said: 'We were looking for a novelty, and *Upstairs, Downstairs* demonstrated there was an audience for the family saga.'

Peter Strauss and Nick Nolte starred as Rudy and Tom Jordache, brothers competing for Julie Prescott (Susan Blakely). Rudy was moving up the establishment ladder; Tom was a trouble maker who was eventually knifed to death. 'Go, get 'em, Rudy – the bad guys,' he ordered his brother as he died, to which Rudy replied: 'I don't know who they are any more; I think I'm one of them.' Then Rudy and Julie sailed tearfully into the sunset, having cast Tom's ashes over the side of his boat.

Producer Jon Epstein said: 'It may not be the greatest thing ever, but it is 18 cuts above average television. The great thing about *Rich Man, Poor Man* is that its success has paved the way for a new kind of programme. This is healthy for us as producers, healthy for actors who love to play complete characters, and healthy for the public who can escape from their usual diet of routine programmes.'

The makers of *Rich Man* immediately commissioned a longer follow-up called *Rich Man, Poor Man, Book Two*, about the surviving brother, Rudy Jordache, as a US senator – even though there was no book from which to adapt it. It was seen in more conventional form as 22 episodes of 50 minutes and it flopped, but by this time other producers, eager as ever to copy a success, were bringing dramatisations of other books to the screen in mini-series form. There was a whole library of them within a few years, including Irwin Shaw's *Evening in Byzantium*, Taylor Caldwell's *Captains and the Kings* and *Testimony of Two Men*, Anton Myrer's *Once an Eagle*, Robert Ludlum's *The Rhinemann Exchange*, Norman Bogner's *Seventh Avenue*, Harold Robbins's *79 Park Avenue*, Arthur Hailey's *Wheels*, Thomas Tryon's *The Dark Secret of Harvest Home*, John Jakes's *The Bastard*, and Howard Fast's *The Immigrants*.

The biggest success of them all was Alex Haley's *Roots*, the saga of a black family from the capture of an African slave in 1767 to the aftermath of the American Civil War. In America its 12 hours were played over eight consecutive nights during a blizzard in 1977. 'The biggest event in TV history,' as it was promoted at the time, was watched in 85 per cent of American homes with television. More than 130 million watched at least some of it; 80 million watched the last episode, then a record for a TV drama. And the impact was nearly as great around the world. It touched the pride of blacks, the consciences of whites. One white woman wrote: '*Roots* has given me another view of coloured people. From now on I will see blacks through different eyes.' Haley said: 'The public has a subconscious hunger for something with weight, depth and social value – and they found it on television in *Roots*'.

It differed from other mini-series in that, while it could be watched like a work of fiction, Haley had based it on 12 years research in which he claimed to have traced his ancestry back seven generations to Kunta Kinte, born in the Gambia in 1750. The story showed Kunta Kinte (played by a young drama student, LeVar Burton) captured by slave traders and shipped with 140 others to be auctioned in Savannah, Georgia. It followed his descendants to 1870 when his grandson, a fighting cock trainer known as Chicken George (Ben Vereen) was emancipated.

Some journalists argued that the evidence about the abduction of Kunta Kinte was weak, but Haley replied: 'Even if I am wrong about what happened in the Gambia, that does not affect the validity of my book. What I have written is a symbolic history of my people. Every black person in America owes his existence to a black person in Africa who was taken across the Atlantic by force. The reason for the book's impact is that it does not start in America like other books on slavery, but in Africa.'

A sequel, *Roots: the New Generation*, in 1979 continued the story to the 1970s, and Haley's arrival in the Gambia to meet members of his ancestral tribe. Haley was played by James Earl Jones, and Marlon Brando appeared in a nine-minute scene as the American Nazi, George Lincoln Rockwell. Brando worked for a nominal fee which he donated to charity and won an Emmy Award.

Steamy and Raunchy

An American producer, Paul Monash, had claimed of *Roots*: 'It shows we can move away from mindless melodrama to stories that have some underlay of meaning.' But in the Eighties, at the height of the popularity of *Dallas* and *Dynasty*, American mini-series came to mean lurid stories about sex, money, power and hedonism, usually in glamorous locations. 'Steamy' and 'raunchy' were the words the tabloids loved to use to describe them.

The Thorn Birds, adapted from a novel by Colleen McCullough, began the trend in 1983. It had a Catholic priest discarding his vows for a romantic fling, and fathering a son. Richard Chamberlain starred as Father Ralph de Bricassart, torn between devotion to his church and love of Meggie Cleary (Rachel Ward), a girl from an Australian sheep station. Captioning a picture still, the London *Daily Mirror* drooled: 'A steamy

All friends at this stage, the Jordache brothers and Julie Prescott in Rich Man, Poor Man.

new TV epic guaranteed to raise viewers' temperatures. . . . The hairy-chested hero is a sexy priest who has just shed his clerical robes to get to grips with a sheep rancher's beautiful daughter.' This set the style for tabloid coverage of further mini-series, the most hyped of which during the following three years were:

Princess Daisy (from a book by Judith Krantz). About the spirited daughter of a polo-playing Russian prince (Stacy Keach) and a Hollywood film star (Lindsay Wagner), both killed in different accidents, and how she became the world's richest model. The title role went to an unknown Danish actress, 22-year-old Merete Van Kemp, after a two-year search and consideration of 700 actresses.

Mistral's Daughter (Judith Krantz again). About a womanising Parisian painter, Mistral (Stacy Keach). Stefanie Powers played Maggie, a Jewish girl who was his model and mistress in the Twenties, and Stephanie Dunham her daughter (by another

Priest and rancher's daughter shed their inhibitions in The Thorn Birds.

man), Teddy, who had an affair with Mistral years later.

Lace (Shirley Conran). About Lili, a Hollywood porn star seeking revenge on her unknown mother for deserting her as a baby. The climax was when Lili (Phoebe Cates) put the question to three women, Pagan (Brooke Adams), who was English, Maxine (Arielle Dombasle), who was French, and Judy (Bess Armstrong), who was American: 'Which one of you bitches is my mother?' (It was Judy.) In *Lace 2* she went on the trail of her unknown father, the man who raped her mother, and asked of King Abdulla of Sydon (Anthony Higgins), German conductor Werner Graff (Patrick Ryecart) and American astronaut Daryl Webster (James Read): 'Which one of you bastards is my father?'

Sins (Judith Gould). About Helen Junot (Joan Collins), an ambitious French model moving from catwalk to boardroom, building the world's most successful magazine empire, while searching for a long-lost brother and the Nazi responsible for her mother's death in World War Two.

Hollywood Wives (Jackie Collins). To quote from the publicity material: 'In this behind-the-scenes look at life among Tinsel Town's moviemakers, power wielders and beautiful people, a major motion picture is being cast, and every actor in Hollywood is vying for a part. While the picture's successful director (Anthony Hopkins), whose wife (Stefanie Powers) wrote the script, is having an affair with a screen sex symbol (Suzanne Somers), determined to secure a part for herself, the devoted spouse (Candice Bergen) of an aging matinée idol (Steve Forrest) puts her own plan into action, and a struggling actor (Andrew Stevens) employs a clever ruse to secure himself a role. Meanwhile, a deranged young man heads for Hollywood to find his real mother. . . .'

On its first showing in Britain the penultimate reel was accidentally omitted. No complaints were recorded.

Lili (Phoebe Cates) right, and the mother she denigrated (Deborah Raffin) in Lace II.

9
The Continuing Stories

Soaps

Coronation Street is the world's longest-running television serial. It began in December 1960 and there have been two half-hour instalments weekly since then, recounting the happenings in the pub, corner shop and terraced houses of a Lancashire street in the shadow of a railway viaduct. Its people have remained unglamorous, unfashionable, mainly working class folk, and it has been widely praised for gritty realism, though it might well be difficult to find a real community like it today. Bill Podmore, long its producer, told me many years ago:

'All over the country, old terraces like Coronation Street are disappearing, but a change in the Street could destroy the roots of the programme, because the architecture is as much a part of its character as the people. The architecture dictates the lifestyle and if you demolish the houses and replace them with a more modern version, then the lives of the characters are affected. Coronation Street could be paved and have little lawns and seats and it would look quite nice, but the present houses are much more interesting than those shoved up by modern architects. It is important to retain the 11 ft by 11 ft room; once you start demolishing walls and making rooms 20 ft wide you could be in any other serial.'

The first episode was transmitted live from Manchester. 'We were all terrified,' recalls William Roache who, as local newspaper editor Ken Barlow, is the only member of the original cast still in the serial. It was originally shown every Friday and Monday, with the Friday episode going out live and the episode for Monday recorded immediately afterwards by the now long obsolete system of telerecording – filming the TV picture from the screen. All programmes have since been videotaped, with film inserts.

Coronation Street was the brainchild of writer Tony Warren, whose first script began with the handing over of the corner shop to a new owner: 'The scene is outside Mrs Lappin's corner shop in Coronation Street. Two girls are playing with a ball and singing. Mrs Lappin comes out with a small boy and puts coin in bubblegum machine, gives gum to boy who walks away. Mrs Lappin looks up at sign which reads MRS LAPPIN – CORNER SHOP, then returns inside where Florrie Lindley is waiting. . . . Mrs Lappin: Now, next thing you've got to do is get a signwriter in. That thing above the door will have to be changed. Florrie: Be funny having my name above me own shop.'

However, the best remembered lines in the first episode were spoken by vinegary-tongued, hairnetted Ena Sharples (Violet Carson), when she entered the shop. 'Are those fancies today's?' she demanded. 'I'll take half a dozen – and no éclairs. *No éclairs.*'

Ena Sharples was to become Britain's first soap superstar, though rivalled by her crony Minnie Caldwell (Margot Bryant), decorative redheaded Elsie Tanner (Patricia Phoenix), Albert Tatlock (Jack Howarth), a grumpy old pensioner, Annie Walker (Doris Speed), the genteel landlady of the Rovers Return, Stan Ogden (Bernard Youens), the Street layabout, and Hilda Ogden (Jean Alexander), his fortune-telling, hair-curlered wife. Many actors who later became famous made their reputations in the Street, among them Arthur Lowe as portly businessman Leonard Swindley.

More than any other serial *Coronation Street* has been believed by many viewers to be fact. When Elsie Tanner was lying unidentified in a London hospital after being knocked down by a taxi, viewers wrote to her husband telling him where she was. When dustman Eddie Yeats (Geoffrey Hughes) had his woolly hat shredded in a washing machine, dozens of viewers sent replacements, and when Ena Sharples was sacked as caretaker of the Glad Tidings Mission, viewers made offers of jobs. At Christmas they try to book rooms in the Rovers Return pub for parties, and whenever a house becomes vacant in the Street viewers beg to rent it.

The storylines, decided at regular conferences of the writers, have mainly concerned such mundane matters as courtships, marriages, births, deaths, celebrations and after-hours drinking in the Rovers, though there have been bigger dramas such as a train crash on the viaduct in 1967 and a fire that destroyed the Rovers Return in 1986. One of the longest and most discussed storylines, which kept viewers on tenterhooks in 1983, was whether Deirdre Barlow (Anne Kirkbride) would leave husband Ken for smooth factory boss Mike Baldwin (Johnny Briggs). She didn't. DEIRDRE AND KEN BACK TOGETHER was flashed on the scoreboard for the crowd at Old Trafford where Manchester United were playing when a reconciliation was revealed on television. Viewers were teased again three years later as to whether Mike Baldwin, having had his fling with Barlow's wife, would marry Barlow's young daughter Susan (Wendy Jane Walker). He did.

Critics warned at the start that *Coronation Street* would never be a hit in the south of England because the lifestyle it portrayed was too alien. Yet by the second half of the Sixties it was not only an institution in

Ken Barlow has a drink with Mike Baldwin, the son-in-law he never wanted, in Coronation Street.

Britain but was being seen in Australia, Canada, New Zealand, Holland, Hong Kong, Nigeria, Singapore and Gibraltar. Since then it has gone into 18 countries in all, and while that does not match the records of other programmes in this book, its influence has been great.

In 1971 a Canadian station in Saskatchewan bought a package of 1,144 episodes – equal to some 23 days and nights of non-stop viewing – in a deal which got into *The Guinness Book of Records* as the biggest single sale of TV programmes. The station bought a further 728 episodes in 1982. The United States was a harder market to break into. Granada offered the serial free in the early Seventies to any American station that would give it a substantial run, but there were no takers, though in 1972 the non-profit-making Public Broadcasting Service ran it for a year, starting at episode 1082.

One can perhaps understand its success in the senior Commonwealth countries with long-standing links with Britain, or in Holland, where the way of life is not so far removed from England's and so many understand English. (Some Dutch children, it is said, have acquired English with a Lancashire accent due to Street-addiction.) It is harder to understand why the Street's gossip and squabbles should interest viewers a world away in Thailand or Nigeria. Harry Kershaw, prolific writer of scripts for the serial, has claimed: 'Coronation Street is about life, and life has its universal situations, its problems and laughter; therefore it has an international appeal.' That seems simplistic, but professors who lecture on Coronation Street and students who write theses about it, have not come up with a better or more succinct explanation.

Peyton Place

It was Coronation Street that was responsible for Peyton Place, the soap that was to lead to 'Dallasty'. In America soaps were traditionally low-budget programmes for daytime viewing, but in the early Sixties

The original cast of Peyton Place *with stars-to-be Mia Farrow and Ryan O'Neal in front.*

American producers cast envious eyes upon the success of the British serial and decided that the USA ought to have a similar twice-weekly prime time soap – although the characters would need to be richer and more glamorous. Their answer was the story of scandalous happenings in a small New England town, developed from a best-selling novel by Grace Metalious and a money-spinning 1957 film starring Lana Turner, though the serial soon went beyond the central characters of the book.

Peyton Place was in production from 1964 to 1969 with two teams under different directors working simultaneously to produce more than 100 episodes a year. Cynical reviewers nicknamed it *Blatant Disgrace*, but it was shown in 50 countries. In Britain, although it was not given a networked slot on ITV – different regions showing it at different times between a year and two years after America – the lives and loves of the Harringtons and Carsons, MacKenzies and Andersons acquired such a fanatical following that tampering with the scheduling caused commotions.

For example, in the south-west of England it was shown at 10.30 pm until elderly people complained that staying up to watch it cost them too much in heating and lighting, so it was moved to 4.25 pm – whereupon 100 women workers in a Plymouth factory demanded time off on two afternoons a week to watch it at the new time. When Thames Television took over weekday ITV programming in London in 1968 and dropped the serial, a bigger storm broke. 'I for one will never watch a serial on commercial television again,' threatened one writer. Another said she was having to rely on letters from a sister in Devon to keep abreast of developments in *Peyton Place*. 'But this is not really satisfactory,' she wrote. 'I am going to give up the lease on my flat and move.' In an East London ship-broking firm 130 workers – a quarter of the staff – signed a petition demanding its return. Thames bowed to the storm and brought it back.

Over five years there were 514 episodes, employing more than 100 actors and actresses and 20 writers – each taking responsibility for the lives of one or more characters. The permanent set grew from a few houses around a square to include shops, a factory, a hospital, a fire station and a wharf, but the intertwining plots and relationships became more and more intricate, and too complex for new viewers, and so it was ended.

In the final scene handsome Dr Mike Rossi (Ed Nelson) faced a murder charge, his alleged victim the ex-husband of his girlfriend Marsha Russell (Barbara Rush). The case was left unresolved. This irritated viewers in Holland, where it topped the ratings, to the extent that the Dutch made their own ending, flying Nelson and Rush to the Netherlands to record it. The ending was a happy one; Rossi was acquitted and he and Marsha Russell fell in each other's arms.

Peyton Place's most celebrated achievement was to make stars out of two unknowns, Mia Farrow and Ryan O'Neal. Farrow, 19 when it began, played the fragile Alison MacKenzie, who disappeared in a fog. O'Neal, 23, blond and boyish, played rich mill owner's son Rodney Harrington. The most established star when *Peyton Place* began was Dorothy Malone, who had won an Oscar for a 1956 film. She played bookstore owner Constance MacKenzie, Alison's mother, while Tim O'Connor played publisher Elliot Carson, Alison's father. Relationships were convoluted. Canadian-born Barbara Parkins was seen as bitchy Betty Anderson Harrington, former wife of Rodney Harrington; Chris Connelly as Norman Harrington, Rodney's younger brother; Patricia Morrow as Rita Jacks Harrington, his wife; Evelyn Scott as waterfront barkeeper Ada Jacks, Rita's mother; James Douglas as drunken lawyer Steven Cord, former husband of Betty Anderson Harrington; and Ruth Warrick as Hannah Cord, the housekeeper who raised him as her son.

The main characters reappeared in 1972 in *Return to Peyton Place*, a daytime soap with an almost entirely different cast, but it failed to recapture the audience and ended after 50 episodes.

Dallas

By tradition soaps had come to mean half-hours screened more than once a week and for 52 weeks in the year, like *Coronation Street* and *Peyton Place*. *Dallas* did not follow that formula, running weekly at 50-minute length with seasonal breaks, yet its name has become synonymous with soap opera. It began in 1978 as a mini-series. Writer David Jacobs had been asked to devise a modern saga and chose Texas because it is big and brash, though he had never been to Dallas. He considered going but was persuaded to wait until he finished writing.

What he devised was the story of a rich Texan family, the Ewings of Southfork ranch; oil and cattle baron Jock and his wife, quaintly known as Miss Ellie, and their children, J.R., Gary and Bobby. 'A family ruthless in its quest for power and passion. Ready to destroy two people who dared defy their own blood for the right to love' ran a pre-screening blurb. That referred to the marriage in New Orleans of Bobby Ewing (Patrick Duffy) and Pamela Barnes (Victoria Principal), for there was a feud between their fathers, rooted in the days when they were partners drilling for oil and Ewing supposedly cheated 'Digger' Barnes (David Wayne).

The mini-series ran a mere five hours, and the *Daily Variety* called it 'A limited series with a limited future', but the serial began five months later. Most of its characters were motivated by lust, greed or envy, but the real star soon emerged as the despicable J.R. Ewing, 'that human oil slick', as *Time* called him, played by Larry Hagman, previously best known as a comedy actor. The shooting of J.R. made newspaper headlines around the world in 1980 and was the start of a tabloid obsession with soaps in which the activities of characters were headlined as though they were real people and took precedence over news of real people. J.R. was shot in his Dallas office in the last programme of the second season, and left fighting for his life in hospital. The question was 'Who shot J.R.?', and bookmakers took bets on the identity of the assailant between the shooting on 26 May and the dénouement in America on 21 Nov. The suspects were many, for he was meant to have more enemies than friends, but the favourites were his wife Sue Ellen, a former Miss Texas

(Linda Gray), his sister-in-law and former mistress, Kristin Shepard (Mary Crosby, daughter of Bing), his brother Bobby, and his business rival Cliff Barnes (Ken Kercheval).

Tee shirts and car stickers proclaimed, 'I shot J.R.', though those of a few individualists declared: 'I don't give a * * * * who shot J.R.'. The would-be killer was eventually revealed as Kristin Shepard, pregnant with J.R.'s child and ordered by him to leave town or face being framed for prostitution. In America 80 million watched the programme; in Britain, where it was seen the following day, the number, according to the BBC, was 27 million.

Dallas was the most popular TV series in the world. Members of the Turkish parliament cut short a meeting to rush home and watch. A ballet in Germany was based on the characters. The Southfork ranch in Texas was visited by as many as 2,000 people a day eager to see the balcony from which J.R. once pushed Kristin into the pool.

Dynasty

In America *Dallas* was networked by CBS, which meant rival ABC needed a still more sudsy soap, and the producer given the task of developing it was Aaron Spelling, maker of *Charlie's Angels*, *The Love Boat* and *Hart to Hart*. The brief handed to writers Esther and Richard Shapiro was to create a larger than life story with sex, drama, gloss, powerful men and beautiful women, and they did. *Dynasty*, which began in 1981 with a three-hour opening episode, was, to quote Esther Shapiro, 'the dramatised fantasy of every middle-aged woman'.

Its original title was *Oil* and it was set in a 48-room mansion in Denver where lived wealthy Blake Carrington. Like Jock Ewing he had obtained his riches from oil, in his case from the Denver-Carrington company's wells in America's south-west, the Middle East and South-East Asia. George Peppard rejected the role; the distinguished-looking John Forsythe took it. The story began with the marriages of Carrington to his secretary Krystle (Linda Evans), and his spoiled daughter Fallon (Pamela Sue Martin) to Jeff Colby (John James).

What was missing in the early episodes was the wickedness J.R. supplied in *Dallas*. The only way of outplaying J.R. was to have a wicked woman, so it was decided to introduce Carrington's ex-wife, Alexis. Sophia Loren was sought for the part but was not interested, so Spelling thought of Joan Collins, good at bitch parts. As Alexis she turned the series around and became a mature sex symbol and also, according to her, the highest paid TV actress in the world. With other stars including Ali MacGraw and Rock Hudson – though Frank Sinatra declined an offer – *Dynasty* became more fashionable than *Dallas*, although it overreached itself in 1985 when it decided that royalty were always good for viewing figures and invented the principality of Moldavia. Amanda Carrington, daughter of Blake and Alexis, became engaged to Prince Michael of Moldavia (Britain's Michael Praed) but it became clear that the producers had been wrong about the appeal of foreign royals and so they were written out with an apparent massacre, Moldavian terrorists mowing down the guests in the church. Alexis was not there, being held a prisoner, according to the story. (Actually Joan Collins was renegotiating her contract.) The question of how many would survive the bloodbath was the end of season cliffhanger intended to trump the shooting of J.R., but when *Dynasty* returned and it transpired that only two had died some fans felt cheated.

At their peaks *Dallas* and *Dynasty* commanded audiences of 100 million in 70 countries. Russians in Estonia tuned to Finnish television transmitters to watch. American hostages in Beirut in 1985 saw their terrorist captors huddled around a television set watching the first series of *Dallas*. The soaps were seen in Zimbabwe and Bangladesh, Israel, Syria and South Africa, and were such important ingredients of schedules that in Britain in 1985 the managing director of an ITV company hijacked *Dallas* from the BBC, which had been screening it, by offering the distributors considerably more money than the BBC had been paying. Unfortunately, this transgressed an unwritten gentleman's agreement that had been observed by ITV and the BBC not to poach such programmes, and a war of words raged until the Independent Broadcasting Authority called upon the ITV company, Thames Television, to find a way of returning *Dallas* to the BBC. This was not a simple matter as a contract had been signed and the distributors were not keen to settle for less than the new price; however, it was eventually accomplished at some cost to Thames and to its managing director, Brian Cowgill, who felt obliged to resign.

Stars of the programmes – filmed 25 minutes apart across Los Angeles – became rich and famous. Hagman's income has been estimated at £5 million a year. Magazine editors promised readers Dallasty-style glamour, and pages of colour were devoted to the men of the soaps, sun-tanned and handsome, and the women in dresses with deep cleavage and hefty shoulder-padding that were copied all over the world. But both series were becoming more implausible. When Barbara Bel Geddes had heart surgery she was replaced as Miss Ellie in *Dallas* by Donna Reed, but when Bel Geddes recovered she took over again. That kind of switch had happened previously in long-running series, but the resurrection of Bobby Ewing was without precedent. Patrick Duffy decided to leave at the end of 1985, so Bobby Ewing was killed in a car accident, saving the life of Pamela. Millions watched him die in hospital after delivering his final words to the assembled Ewings: 'Be a family.' They saw his body lowered into its grave. However, fans missed him and Duffy missed *Dallas* and agreed to return. After the writers had agonised fruitlessly about how he could be reintroduced, the return was accomplished simply. Pamela was on honeymoon, having married Mark Graison when – in the most notorious shower scene since *Psycho* – Bobby called from the shower, asking to be handed a towel. All that had gone before was explained away as just a bad dream by his wife; Bobby had never died.

Dynasty, too, was unafraid of the improbable. When Pamela Sue Martin wanted to leave *Dynasty* the character of Fallon was written out in a plane crash, but after second thoughts it was explained that she had not been aboard the plane, had suffered amnesia and wandered America. She had certainly

Blake Carrington (John Forsythe) and his bride Krystle Jennings (Linda Evans) in Dynasty.

changed, for the part had been taken over by Emma Samms, 14 years younger, three inches shorter and English. Later Fallon was to be kidnapped by aliens from outer space who bundled her into a space ship after her car stalled on a deserted road. When she returned she told husband Jeff the space ship smelled of cinnamon. 'Were they baking?' he inquired.

That was in *Dynasty 2*; *The Colbys*, a spin-off in 1985, about a branch of the Carrington family which had Charlton Heston as Jason Colby, Barbara Stanwyck as Constance Colby Patterson, and Katharine Ross as Jeff Colby's mother, Francesca Scott Colby Hamilton – although the actress was hardly old enough to be his mother. Britain's Stephanie Beacham, who had starred as a glamorous bitch in *Connie*, was imported to play Sable Colby, and do for it what Joan Collins had done for *Dynasty*.

Dallas had already launched a spin-off in 1979 in *Knots Landing*, about Gary Ewing (Ted Shackleford), California-based brother of J.R. and Bobby, and his wife Valene (Joan Van Ark). This was followed in 1981 by *Falcon Crest*, made by the same producers as *Dallas*, about a family named Channing, owners of vineyards in the Napa Valley. But in the second half of the Eighties the great soap bubble appeared to have burst and audiences began to decline.

10
Super-
animation

Cartoons and Puppets

Fred Flintstone and his wife Wilma enjoyed the lifestyle of the 20th century in the Stone Age in *The Flintstones*. Their home was a luxury split-level cave (345 Stone Cave Road) in the town of Bedrock, where Fred worked as a dino (dinosaur) operator for the Slaterock Gravel Co. They kept up with the news in *The Daily Slate* which was printed on stone slabs, and went to the supermarket in their convertible car which had stylish fins, solid rock wheels and a thatched roof top. Their hi-fi, which played grooved discs of rock, used a sharp-beaked bird as the stylus; their vacuum cleaner was a baby elephant on roller skates, its trunk serving as the hose, and their tin-opener was a lizard with a buck tooth.

Fred and Wilma, and their neighbours, Barney and Betty Rubble, were created in 1960 by Bill Hanna and Joe Barbera, who made *Tom and Jerry* cartoons for the cinema in the Thirties. Later they set up a TV factory to turn out economical, 'semi-animated' (meaning limited movement) cartoons, beginning with *Huckleberry Hound* and *Yogi Bear* in 1958, but *The Flintstones* was their first cartoon series meant for peak viewing time. Barbera said:

'There was so much adult acceptance of these shows we decided to try an adult cartoon series. Bill and I tried out something like six different families in contemporary settings but somehow they didn't fit the bill. Then we hit on the idea of taking an average couple, happily married, with the trials and

happenings of everyday living, and putting them in a Stone Age setting.'

Hanna expanded on that:

'Trying out our ideas we drew our couple in modern atmosphere in a car – no laugh. But when we drew them in a caveman car we all laughed. Then we drew a regular guy at a piano; again, no laugh. So we drew him in caveman attire in a cave dwelling, plunking away at a stone piano – a Stoneway grand, naturally. The result was hilarious.'

All-action Puppets

One-dimensional cartoons have since been outstripped in popularity by television programmes featuring puppets, and Britain's Gerry Anderson created some of the most advanced, with his *Supercar, Fireball XL5* and *Stingray* leading to *Thunderbirds* in 1966. The adventures of Jeff Tracy's International Rescue squad that would fly anywhere to avert a disaster, became cult viewing for many adults as well as children. It was the first hour-long puppet film series to be made for television and combined 20-inch high puppets on wires one 5,000th of an inch thick with intricate tabletop models of bridges, skyscrapers, airports and rocket launching sites.

There were five Thunderbird machines. *Thunderbird 1* was a silver-grey, 7,000 mph scout vehicle with vertical take-off and landing capability, booster rockets and retractable wings, which was piloted by Scott, the oldest of Jeff Tracy's sons. Its function

Self-propelled golf cart, Stone Age style. On the links in The Flintstones.

was to be first on the scene when a rescue was mounted and to serve as a mobile operations control centre. *Thunderbird 2*, piloted by the reliable Virgil, was a green freighter with rollers instead of wheels, which was designed to carry heavy and ingenious rescue equipment including a two-seater Mole which could burrow under-ground. To discharge its cargo the main fuselage of the freighter lifted on hydraulic telescopic legs.

Thunderbird 3, piloted by the impetuous Alan, was orange and capable of flying into space, and *Thunderbird 4*, controlled by the young and enthusiastic Gordon, was a yellow underwater scout craft carried in *Thunderbird 2*. All these craft were based at International Rescue's secret headquarters, inside a mountain on a remote Pacific island where nature had been adapted to aid secrecy. The cliff face moved, trees fell back and a swimming pool disappeared so that the craft could enter and leave their hiding

A 20-inch-tall puppet on wires – but a real hero to young viewers of The Thunderbirds.

places. *Thunderbird 5*, piloted by the patient John, remained on the alert in space.

Other members of the team included Brains, a bespectacled scientific genius who invented all the machines and equipment, and Lady Penelope, the organisation's elegant blonde London agent, who travelled in a shocking pink Rolls-Royce with the registration number FAB 1, driven by Parker, her Cockney chauffeur, who was a reformed safe-blower. Frequently they tangled with a villain known as the Hood, a master of disguise who lived in an Eastern temple and whose eyes lit up when he cast spells. He was a half-brother of Jeff Tracy's servant, Kyrano, whose daughter Tin-Tin was an

electronics expert. *Thunderbirds* was one of the most heavily merchandised programmes of its day, with toys, comics and records.

Kermit and Company

There were no strings to the puppets in *Sesame Street* which adapted the techniques of TV commercials to prepare small children for the transition to school. Produced by Joan Ganz Cooney through her Children's Television Workshop, a non-profit-making educational corporation in New York, it began in 1969 as an hour-long show five days a week on the Public Broadcasting Service. It has since been shown in more than 50 countries in its original form, and there have also been local language editions in Germany, France and Holland.

It was aimed mainly at three- to five-year-olds in low income and under-privileged families – hence the setting of a street in Harlem – and used cartoons, puppets, films and live performances to familiarise them with letters of the alphabet and numbers. As in commercials, items were rarely longer than 30 seconds in duration. Joan Ganz Cooney said: 'When we first started people said, "How do you know TV can teach?" And I said, "Well, I hear every child in America singing beer commercials. If television can do that why can't it do something more constructive?" '

Research was extensive, both before and after the launch. Social scientists watched the impact of programmes on children in day care nurseries, and numerous films and cartoons were discarded as a result. Dr Edward Palmer, research director of the Workshop, said:

'We've learned that even tots of this age are quite selective. Their interest is turned on and off on a moment-to-moment basis. The set may be on but it doesn't always have their attention. What bores them particularly is too much time being spent on any one subject. They like variety and frequent changes of scenes. Nothing loses them faster than an adult full-face on the screen just talking. Even at this age they don't like to be lectured, it seems.'

So a *Sesame Street* programme might contain as many as 50 different short items, but the undoubted stars from the start were the Muppets, a diverse band of furry monsters, humanoids and animals who clowned and introduced 30-second cartoons, films and live performances. The Muppets (named from a combination of the words, marionettes and puppets) had been devised by Jim Henson, a puppeteer for more than 20 years, and they had appeared regularly on *Sam and Friends*, a TV show in Washington, before they went to New York where they were guests in shows starring Perry Como, Bob Hope and Julie Andrews. Some of the *Sesame Street* Muppets already had a long history – like Kermit the Frog who was born in 1954 when Henson made him from an old coat of his mother's, a table tennis ball and some cardboard – though most were created specially for *Sesame Street* and made of a type of foam rubber. They included Big

Bird, a naive 8 ft-tall canary which nested in the streets, Oscar the Grouch, living morosely in a dustbin, Ernie and Bert Snuffle-Upagus, two parts elephant and one part anteater in appearance, who could not be seen by adults on the show, and Sam the robot, a machine with a mind of its own.

From the educationalists' point of view their appeal cut across ethnic, social and economic bounds. 'The only kids who can identify along racial lines with the Muppets have to be either green or orange,' Henson joked.

Hensen went on to develop his characters further for *The Muppet Show* in 1976. The idea had been rejected by the big American networks (as *Sesame Street* had been) but Sir Lew Grade liked it, so *The Muppet Show* was made in Britain in studios at Boreham Wood, Herts. The 300 puppets in the series hung in rows around a workshop there beneath a notice warning: 'Please do not fondle, molest, handle, touch or tweak the puppets'. They were mostly made in America of foam rubber with fur fabric trimmings, and the majority of them were glove puppets, though there were also wooden-framed giants which sat on the puppeteers' shoulders.

Each programme took a week to record on a stage 20 ft wide. Henson and the other operators were below it with their arms in the air, right hand in the puppet's head to move its mouth, left hand operating the puppet's left arm. (To move a Muppet's other arm a second puppeteer was needed.) The puppeteers also provided the voices of their charges, Henson speaking the lines of Kermit, among others, and they wore head-sets to amplify their voices and receive messages from the director, for their only view of the stage and what was happening above their heads was on television monitor screens.

The programmes concerned the making and presenting of variety shows, directed and compèred by Kermit, his most temperamental star being Miss Piggy, a blonde, porcine femme fatale with a good left hook. She was in love with the frog, and would coo at him: 'Kissy, kissy'. Other performers included Fozzie Bear, an incompetent comic, Rowlf, a shaggy, piano-playing dog, the Great Gonzo, a hooked-beaked stunt artist, and Sweetums, an amiable but ugly 9 ft-tall monster. Barracking came from Sam, an American eagle, defender of the uplifting and decent, who denounced every show as 'weird', and aged humanoid hecklers Statler and Waldorf, who were always to be found in a box at the theatre, hating every act. The Muppets also had impressive human guests. Rudolf Nureyev danced a *pas de deux* from *Swan Lake* with Miss Piggy, and Peter Sellers, as a mad German osteopath, tied a pig in knots. Elton John sang *Crocodile Rock* with a chorus of reptilian Muppets, and Roger Moore, Raquel Welch, James Coburn, Lena Horne, Peter Ustinov and George Burns were among others who braved working with them.

Satirical Puppets

Puppets could also be used to guy the famous, as *Spitting Image* has demonstrated with some of the cruellest and most irreverent satire since *That Was the Week That Was* in the Sixties. Politicians, royalty, sports personalities and show business stars, represented by unflattering effigies, were featured in ludicrous situations. President Reagan was seen being trounced at chess by his dog, Lucky, and Prime Minister Margaret Thatcher was seen thumping rowdies in her Cabinet with a straight left between the eyes.

When the series began in 1984 viewers enthused about the puppets, the work of Peter Fluck and Roger Law, but rubbished the scripts. 'Great puppets, lousy show' was a common complaint, echoing the words of Conservative politician Norman Tebbit, after being depicted as a skinhead in a leather bomber jacket and jeans: 'The puppets are marvellous but the scripts are puerile.' Some of the complaints were occasioned by the preponderance of political sketches; many viewers were unable to recognise the targets of them, and it was difficult to find enough topical material each week. This led to sketches, and speeches within them, being over long, with the result that viewers realised that puppet faces could not provide the subtlety of expressions of humans, and became hypnotised watching the synchronisation, or lack of it, between voices and latex lips. Sketches were eventually made shorter, the political content was reduced and the proportion of show business spoofs increased; *Spitting Image* then acquired a cult following, and American television commissioned special shows.

However, scurrilous representations of the Royal Family, particularly perhaps of Prince Charles who was depicted as jug-eared and wet, offended many, even though the makers claimed their lampoons were meant affectionately. The royal reaction was unknown; when asked, a Palace spokesman stonewalled: 'I'm not saying they watch it, and I'm not saying they don't. We've been directed to make no comment.' Producer John Lloyd's attitude to complaints was:

'We are no great respecters of people in high positions. We reckon that our leaders have to earn respect from the public. It's not compulsory to admire them simply because they've got where they have. One of the wonderful advantages of living in Britain, of course, is that a satirical programme like ours is allowed to be made.'

No one in the public eye was safe from mockery by the preposterous puppets and the words put into their mouths, which were spoken by a team of versatile mimics. Jan Ravens, for example, provided voices for the Queen, the Queen Mother, Princess Diana and television presenter Esther Rantzen; Jessica Martin spoke for Dolly Parton and Barbra Streisand; John Glover for Prince Philip, athlete Daley Thompson, newscaster Sir Alastair Burnet and South Africa's P.W. Botha; Chris Barrie for Ronald Reagan, Prince Andrew and Labour Party leader Neil Kinnock.

The words themselves were left until the last moment in the interests of topicality; a new puppet could be made in a week. All of them were made in London from modelling clay, glass fibre and latex, the floppy latex skin covering a glass fibre half-skull. Each puppet required the services of three handlers, one animating the mouth by gripping the inner foam rubber, the others squeezing bulbs that operated eyeball and eyelid mechanisms. It could take an hour to film a sketch lasting 90 seconds, and the time involved made *Spitting Image* possibly the most expensive light entertainment show on British television – despite having no human stars to pay.

11
A World of Entertainment
Comedy, Song and Dance

Benny Hill is the most famous comedian in the world, known through television in 80 countries from Cuba to Cyprus and Swaziland to Sri Lanka. He has been a favourite on British TV since the start of the Sixties, and achieved international fame in 1979 when a number of his hour-long shows made over 10 years were re-edited into half-hours omitting totally indigenous references, and sold to America. The Americans took to his sex-obsessed humour; his programmes were screened twice nightly on some stations, and there was a near riot at a penitentiary in California when the local station moved *The Benny Hill Show* to 11.30 pm, half an hour after 'lights out'. Apart from Russia, few countries have since resisted his leering, winking comedy. He has been seen even in China, though that country is selective and rejects what is considered too risqué. 'No comic since Chaplin or Stan Laurel has spanned the world like he has,' says Philip Jones, head of light entertainment at Thames Television, which made *The Benny Hill Shows*.

Few comedians have come even near, for joke shows rarely travel. One was Jack Benny, whose surname Hill adopted as his first in place of Alfred, with which he was christened. Jack Benny was one of television's first comics, moving from radio at the start of the Fifties, and appearing in some 350 shows with Mary Livingstone, his wife, Eddie Anderson as his valet, Rochester, and Mel Blanc as his violin

teacher. His jokes about his stinginess and his violin playing made him rich enough to buy a Stradivarius which he played with symphony orchestras for charity. His closest rival of the time was George Burns, two years younger, who appeared with his wife Gracie Allen in *The Burns and Allen Show*.

However, the comedy of both Benny and Burns was mainly verbal, which suffers in translation. Hill's is largely visual. The podgy comic is seen as a dirty old man pursuing gorgeous girls – though never achieving any success with them. The lightly clothed nymphets, Hill's Angels, are also able to be appreciated in all countries, though some such as the Gulf States have declined to screen the programmes because of what is known as their 'jiggle factor'. Hill says: 'We traverse language barriers because there is so much visual comedy. A man in Afghanistan – and I'm not sure whether we're shown there or not – can watch the show and understand a lot of it. Only about 30 per cent of my viewers live in Britain.'

The main ingredients are blue sketches and songs derived from old jokes, delivered with a saucy grin. These give offence to many, and have been denounced as sexist and smutty – not only by women – though Hill, who has never married, regards them as being in the same tradition as bawdy postcards at the seaside. He writes his own material and this is one reason he makes only three new hour-long shows a year and never performs on stage. The others, he readily admits, are that he likes spending his time travelling and lounging in the sun. He has no need to work for he has made more than 50 one-hour shows over 16 years, which have been packaged into more than 80 half-hour programmes. He has, however, made commercials for many countries which have screened his shows, promoting beer in Greece, biscuits in France, television sets in Spain and stores in Australia.

Catchphrases

Like most comics of his generation, Hill learned his trade in variety shows, and at one time these were a staple of television. The first television comedy show born of the electronic age rather than being merely an updated version of music hall was *Laugh-In* which began in 1968 and was the fastest, liveliest and most original comedy show of its day. A tightly-edited mix of short skits and one-liners, it flashed backwards and forwards, using black-outs and quick cuts, and influenced light entertainment all round the world.

It made millionaires of the two hosts, Dick Martin, playing the idiot, and Dan Rowan, his suntanned, moustached, straight man, partners in comedy for more than a quarter of a century, who always signed off with a routine lifted from Burns and Allen:

Rowan: 'Say goodnight, Dick.'

Martin: 'Goodnight, Dick.'

No show ever produced more catch-phrases than *Laugh-In*. 'Is this the party to whom I am speaking?' asked Lily Tomlin every week as Ernestine, a snobbish, nasal switchboard operator. 'I forgot the question,' pouted Goldie Hawn as the archetypal dumb blonde. 'Verrry interesting ... but stupid!' sneered Arte Johnson as a steel-helmeted German soldier behind a potted plant. Others included Dick Martin's 'I'll drink to that,' and 'You bet your sweet bippy!', 'Hi, sports fans,' from Alan Sues as a TV sports presenter, and 'Here come de judge,' announced by 'Pigmeat' Markham. Most famous of the catchphrases, however, was 'Sock it to me!', spoken by British actress Judy Carne. Whenever she used it she would be hit by a bucket of water, or get a custard pie in the face.

Guest stars were sometimes induced to

Dan Rowan and Dick Martin, hosts of Laugh-In, *influential comedy show of the Sixties.*

say this last line, though they were rarely subjected to similar indignities. Richard Nixon, running for the American Presidency in 1968, complied – six times, in fact, during recording, because he could not get the inflection right. (For political balance, the same opportunity was offered to his Democratic rival, Hubert Humphrey, who declined.) Sammy Davis Jr appeared on the show several times but every time he began to sing he was dropped through a trap door. John Wayne walked on to utter the one line, 'Well, I don't think that is funny,' and other guests included Mae West, Jack Lemmon, Jimmy Durante and Kirk Douglas.

Every show opened with announcer Gary Owens, hand cupped to ear, declaring: 'This is beautiful downtown Burbank', that being the location of the NBC studios where the show was recorded. Regular features included a cocktail party scene, the Flying Fickle Finger of Fate award (a prize in a mock

Sir John Gielgud as butler and Joan Collins as titled lady in one of the Tales of the Unexpected.

Overleaf *Playing Christ on the screen is a challenge, but Robert Powell was mesmeric in* Jesus of Nazareth.

talent contest), and a joke wall in which the cast opened and shut windows to call one-liners. *Laugh-In* had no political platform. It joked about serious issues but was not trying to change the world, nor was it cruel, though it was sometimes outrageous by the standards of its time. One item in its regular feature, News of the Future, read:

'Dateline: the Vatican 1988. With marriage in the Church now an accepted practice, the Archbishop and his lovely bride, the former Sister Mary Catherine, both announced that this time it's for keeps – if only for the sake of the children.'

Dan Rowan claimed 'We got past the censors by being so fast they didn't know what the jokes meant.' However, some gags were banned. One had a girl saying, 'Don't talk to me about the Pill. It not only doesn't work but it keeps falling out!'

Bloopers

Murphy's Law, as quoted in television circles, holds that if anything *can* go wrong it will go wrong – on air – and *It'll Be Alright on the Night*, an occasional series since 1977, was based on that law, a compilation of gaffes and duff film out-takes from TV and movies, strung together wittily by Denis Norden who says: 'Any Tom, Dick or Harry placed in front of a camera can become a Wally.' In clips rescued from waste bins, dancers were seen tripping over scenery, actors falling off sofas during love scenes, and a cookery demonstrator finding her oven on fire.

Memorable moments included a female singer bursting out of her strapless costume, an actor offering a friend a light for a cigarette and sticking the flaming match up his nose, an actress answering a telephone phone before it rang, and – Norden's own favourite – an interviewer given a ferret to hold during a conversation. The camera showed it gradually sinking its teeth into his hand while the interviewer, squirming in agony, strove bravely to pretend the speaker had his full attention. But as Norden has said:

'We're not in the business of making people feel humiliated or hurt and we never put anything in without getting the per-mission of *everyone* who appears on the screen. We've even employed a detective agency to trace people who featured in street interviews.'

To obtain the material the production team have advertised in show business trade papers and contacted television organisations around the world. Norden again:

'To find a prince you've got to kiss an awful lot of frogs. It's the same with finding funny out-takes. You've got to look through an awful lot of them. For one programme we watched 28 hours of them and most last only 15 seconds or so. I recommend watching four hours of Japanese out-takes in Japanese. That works as well as any sedative.'

That also accounts for *Alright on the Night* being only an occasional series rather than a weekly one, but it has led to America developing at least five similar 'blooper shows', as they are called in the USA.

All the Way to the Bank

In song and dance shows *The Perry Como Show* of the Fifties set the style for years ahead. Como was the highest paid enter-tainer on television, crooning his way through hits such as *Catch a falling star* and *Magic moments*, usually dressed in casual knitwear and totally relaxed. He was, in fact, so relaxed that a joke of the time went:

'*Did you see Perry Como?*'
'No. I fell asleep.'
'*So did he!*'

The shows spanned the Fifties, after which he appeared only in occasional specials, particularly at Christmas, filmed in different countries of the world.

A startling contrast to the golfing sweaters of Como were the stage costumes affected by Liberace. The pianist, previously known as Walter Busterkeys, whose shows were in mass production throughout the Fifties and Sixties, wore the most flamboyant clothes on the box. He had a gold lamé tailcoat made by Dior, sequinned suits, a tuxedo with diamond buttons spelling out his name, and another with 24 carat gold braid which he wore with silver kneeboots. He had a chinchilla cape and a fox fur coat with a floor-sweeping 12 ft train, though he sur-passed this in the televised Royal Command Performance of 1978 by appearing in a reproduction of George the Fifth's coronation robes. On one hand he frequently wore a ring in the form of a miniature piano studded with 50 diamonds; the other hand boasted a whole cluster of rings. He performed on a glass-topped piano on which stood electric candelabra.

'He was to serious music what popular newspapers are to news,' wrote *The Times* obituarist on his death in 1987. He edited classics down to between four and six minutes. The *Moonlight Sonata* got four. He also sang nasally and tap danced clumsily. On one occasion he featured an actress dressed as a nun while he played *Ave Maria*. He simpered and dimpled and extolled his mother to audiences in a clotted cream voice. 'What a wonderful thing it would be if we stopped to say, "I love you" to everybody every day,' he burbled.

He was an entertainer one either loved or loathed. In 1959 the *Daily Mirror* columnist Cassandra (William Connor) described him venomously as 'a deadly, winking, sniggering, snuggling, chromium plated, scent-impregnated, luminous, quivering, giggling, fruit-flavoured, mincing, ice-covered heap of mother love'. The pianist sued for libel, won and donated the damages to cancer research. Generally, however, he laughed at jibes. After savage criticism he retorted: 'I cried all the way to the bank – and then I bought the bank.' He did, in fact, own a bank.

Dean Martin, whose series began in 1965, brought a return to the casual style. He would stroll on to the studio floor before a show, drawing attention to the glass in his hand. 'I've been stoned more times than the embassies,' he would joke, though the glass actually contained ginger ale. He would launch into a string of warm-up jokes about booze and broads and what Sammy Davis Jr said to the rabbi. He would sing a few bars: 'Hello young lovers, you're under arrest.' Then he would hoist himself on to a stool for the show, reading his lines from large 'idiot boards' and making gags about them.

For his fat contract he worked one day a week. He had warned the studio: 'I don't want to spend 60 hours a week in rehearsal and conference . . . that's not my style.' So he would arrive in mid-morning, rehearse until 4.30, and by 9 pm would be on his way home, the show recorded.

We are Family – The Osmonds smile for the camera.

His contract, however, was outclassed by the £9 million deal Sir Lew Grade signed with Tom Jones in 1968. This was to make 17 shows a year for five years for Britain's ATV and America's ABC. *This Is Tom Jones* was claimed to be the biggest and most expensive musical series produced in Britain, and the Welsh singer's share of the deal was worth nearly £1 million a year. Only four years earlier he had been earning £15 a week on a building site, although he said: 'A million pounds a year sounds ridiculous, but it has come along gradually, and it's not that I keep anything like a million after tax and expenses.'

The miner's son who became a star with *It's Not Unusual* and *The Green Green Grass of Home* – big, loud songs delivered in a virile baritone with thrusting hip movements – went on to become an international star, and he knew the reason:

'Mature women like to get a bit of a charge now and again. When they see me coming out on the stage like an animal they know what I'm about. I'm trying to get across to the audience that I'm alive. All of it – the emotion and the sex and the power, the heartbeat and the bloodstream – are all theirs for the asking.'

Idols of the Teenyboppers

Grade followed up by signing Engelbert Humperdinck and Julie Andrews to make series in Hollywood. As Gerry Dorsey, Humperdinck had been living on £8 a week national assistance only three years earlier; Andrews, of course, was the established star of *The Sound of Music*. What they had in common, and shared with most singers on television, was that they appealed to family audiences. Television had generally provided little intended specifically for teenagers, but in the mid-Sixties, the era of the Beatles, they could not be ignored. Inspired by the success of the Beatles' films, *A Hard Day's Night* and *Help!*, two American producers conceived the idea of a television show based on the adventures of a pop group. This required a quartet of actors capable of playing pop performers, so they advertised in *Daily Variety*: 'MADNESS! Auditions – folk and rock 'n' roll musicians/ singers. Running parts for four insane boys, ages 17 to 21, with the courage to work.'

They interviewed 437 would-be rock stars from among the respondents and chose David Jones, a Manchester-born 5 ft 3 in actor, Peter Tork, a part-time musician from Washington, Mike Nesmith, who was playing guitar in the coffee houses of Los Angeles, and Mickey Dolenz, lead singer in a Californian group. The new group was first called the Turtles, then the Inevitables, and finally *The Monkees*, which also became the title of the series in 1966.

The pilot programme was recorded with deliberate use of out-of-focus and underlit and overlit scenes. The musical content was played, not by the four, but by experienced studio musicians. Some stations were unhappy about screening it because of the boys' long hair, but publicists went to work to hype the series. There was a distribution of car bumper stickers reading. 'Monkee Business is Big Business'. Six thousand disc

The Monkees – *the pop group that was created for television in 1966.*

jockeys were sent Monkees records, and three days before transmission of the first programme a single, *Last Train to Clarksville*, with Dolenz singing lead, was released. After the first TV show it went to number one in the charts.

The popularity of the group waned when word spread that the stars did not actually do the playing on their hit records, but they were eventually competent enough to play concert dates. They visited England in 1968 and not since the Beatles had last passed through had London Airport heard such screaming. They finally broke up in 1970, only Nesmith continuing as a soloist. Dolenz, who became a producer and director in England (notably of the children's series *Metal Mickey*) said: 'We proved ourselves. OK, we were a manufactured group but the chemistry of our learning did create something which has lasted.'

As the Monkees were bowing out in 1970 the Partridges opened their doors. *The Partridge Family* was the story of a widow and her five children living in San Pueblo, California, who were organised into a rock group by Danny, the 10-year-old. The music was again pre-recorded before the cast came to the studios. The mother was played by Shirley Jones, who had been an established musical star since the movie of *Oklahoma!* in 1955, but the discovery was 20-year-old David Cassidy, who played her 16-year-old son, Keith. The son of actor Jack Cassidy, he was actually Jones's stepson.

His first hit with the Partridge family, *I think I love you*, sold more than five million records. The series went on to amass seven gold discs for albums and five for singles. Cassidy became the idol of the teenyboppers. He promoted bubblegum and toothpaste; his face was on cornflake packets. 'I used to work seven days a week,' he has said. 'On weekdays I worked from 7 am to 7 pm shooting, then from 7.30 pm to midnight recording, and at weekends I'd do concerts.' He enjoyed, it was said, wall-to-wall discs and kerb-to-kerb girls. In 1975 he retired, aged 24, to breed horses on his ranch.

The search for young stars went on, and in 1976 resulted in *Donny and Marie*, Donny Osmond, 18, and his sister Marie, 16, had been in show business all their lives

as members of the Osmonds, a clean-living, God-fearing, Mormon family of six toothy, white-suited boys and one toothy, white-frocked girl. They were the antithesis of the rebellious, long-haired, drug-experimenting rock stars detested by the elderly; they looked sparkling clean, flashed cute smiles, espoused Mormon beliefs such as no smoking, swearing, drinking or pre-marital sex, and were pledged to obey their parents and give a tenth of their income to the church. This endeared them more to the elderly than to teenagers.

For the series a new production complex was built in Salt Lake City, so that big ice-skating numbers could be featured in the shows which the siblings hosted, but after three years they went their own ways and Donny admitted: 'It was stressful; we didn't fight but there were times when we just didn't want to see each other.'

Curiously, although dancing is a visual art, it has featured in few series that have achieved an international audience. An exception was *Fame* in 1982, about the problems of pupils at a New York dancing school, which was modelled on the High School for the Performing Arts in Manhattan, although many of the rooms were re-created in studios in Los Angeles. The series stemmed from a 1980 film directed by Alan Parker. Debbie Allen, a 5 ft 2 in black dancer, had only two lines in that, but carried major responsibility for the television series, for on screen she starred as Lydia Grant, a demanding dance teacher, and off screen she was the show's choreographer. She declared:

'The show isn't just about being on a stage. It's about kids who have a commitment to achieving a goal, and I believe that appeals to something that crosses all geographic boundaries to the energy and passion in people. Success isn't just money, it isn't just recognition. It's work, a lot of work, seven days a week, every week.'

The series, which also brought fame to Gene Anthony Ray, as Leroy, a lithe native of Harlem, was probably more popular in other countries than in America; it was a sensation in Britain at the time production ended, after which the cast went on a stage tour.

Gene Anthony Ray as frenetic, elastic-limbed dancer Leroy Johnson in Fame.

12
The Real World

Current Affairs and Documentaries

It is not true that *World in Action* producers chew nails and spit rust, but they have never done anything to discourage the impression. In fact, down the years they have nurtured their image as the hairy-chested Hemingways of current affairs TV. In pursuit of stories *World in Action* men have posed as arms dealers in Geneva and hippo hunters in Zimbabwe. They have smuggled film from behind the Iron Curtain. They have had a cameraman shot in Jordan, a producer beaten up in Uganda and a reporter jailed in Austria. None of this is unprecedented in current affairs television but *World in Action* has managed to make it seem like a way of life.

With its dramatic style of presentation, underlined by aggressive commentaries delivered by a voice over, it has long been the most sensational and hardest-hitting current affairs series on the screen. It has ranged the world in search of material, three out of ten programmes being made abroad, and they have been seen in 107 countries, almost twice as many as the rival *This Week*, though some broadcasting authorities tend to be selective about those that they buy. Communist countries, for example, tend to pick programmes that show unpleasant aspects of the West.

World in Action has tussled with authority – from its masters at the Independent Broadcasting Authority to the high courts. It was *World in Action* which provided a long running news story in 1980 by refusing to name a British Steel mole who had supplied confidential documents for a programme that embarrassed the Corporation during a steel strike.

'Show a *World in Action* man a windmill and he will tilt at it almost by reflex action,' claimed a former executive producer of the series, and it is a long-standing joke at Granada that a history of the programme is to be written under the title, *How to Lose Friends and Influence People*.

It was 1963 when the first show reached the screen – without any advance publicity because Granada chiefs regarded it as an experiment which might flop. Its competition was well established; the BBC's *Panorama* had been running since 1953, and ITV's *This Week* since 1956. *World in Action* was to be different. It was created by and took its style from Tim Hewat, a restless Australian newspaperman. Alex Valentine, who worked with him and later succeeded him as executive producer, has written: 'Hewat was not renowned for subtlety of speech or manner. "Direct" was a word often carefully chosen to describe his approach.'

That is understatement of a kind not usually associated with the series. Hewat was forceful and his language would have made Alf Garnett wince. He had little time for the conventional current affairs style. Conventionally, reporters talked to viewers from the scene of a story. 'Who wants to see the bloody reporter?' demanded Hewat. Conventionally, benevolent link-men fronted programmes. 'Too bloody cosy,' said Hewat. Conventionally, balance was achieved by studio discussions. 'Talking heads belong on bloody radio,' said Hewat.

It was too easy, he claimed, to make programmes saying, 'On the one hand . . . and on the other.' He wanted clarity. So the on-screen reporter, the anchorman and the studio discussion were out as far as *World in Action* was concerned, replaced by dramatic film, interviewees talking directly to viewers (the interviewer having been edited out) and a forthright commentary to push the show along.

The first programme in 1963 was about the atomic arms race, and Hewat had actors playing John F. Kennedy and Nikita Krushchev scowling at each other through a forest of model missiles. As other programmes followed, the series was called brash, strident, raucous, opinionated and many other things, but its impact was undeniable.

Hewat had established a completely self-contained unit with its own labs and viewing room in Granada's London headquarters. He had no office of his own; he worked at a table in the main room, accessible to all and with all accessible to him. His weekly planning conferences were attended by the whole team, even the dark room boy being encouraged to have his say. 'Democratically decided,' he would declare, taking a vote on an idea.

However, Hewat was not always so willing to let democracy prevail. When typhoid broke out in Zermatt, Switzerland, at the height of the ski season, he proposed covering it in the next programme. Six days, he calculated, were sufficient for *World in Action* to get there, film, return, edit and screen the material. Everyone else was against the idea, but Hewat declared. 'This is a dictatorship', and next day arrived in Zermatt with a camera team, 27 bottles of wine and 60 bars of chocolate. (He had been warned not to touch the local food or water.)

Members of the team were the only people arriving; everyone else was trying to get out, and the team was not welcome, for Zermatt was seeking to play down the outbreak. Villagers pelted the camera crew

An Ulster Volunteer Force leader interviewed by World in Action *in 1972.*

with rocks, but they filmed their story and screened it as scheduled.

Hewat later returned to Australia to edit a newspaper but the programme has found equally determined successors, and while, over the years, it has on occasion used front men and reporters on screen, and even studio discussions, the archetypal format has remained the narrative with voice over.

Heavy research is commonplace. For a programme about ballot rigging during elections in Guyana, *World in Action* hired 24 theology students to check whether 44,000 Guyanese voters said to be living in Britain were genuine. They found that in London only one in six existed; in Manchester only one in 20. More typically, a researcher spent five months in Italian cities in 1976 amassing

103

25 files of evidence about allegations of payola – specifically that major oil companies got together to induce Italian politicians to pass favourable legislation, then paid back a percentage of their gains to party funds.

Research can be lengthy. An exposure of corruption in Hong Kong took four years to complete. *The Betrayal of Bhopal*, an award-winning investigation into the chemical plant leak in India which killed 2,500, took six months to make. The greatest difficulty is inevitably getting material on film. *World in Action* has frequently filmed clandestinely from the back of a car. Probing arms deals in Switzerland, a cameraman hid in a car to film a meeting between an arms dealer and producer Jeremy Wallington, who was posing as a man with three British frigates for sale. Wallington guided the dealer to a seat in the window of a hotel bar and filming began, but the cameraman thought he had been spotted when the dealer pointed directly at him. Actually, Wallington told him later, the dealer was drawing attention to the way the car was being rocked by the wind.

World in Action has also employed stake-outs. During an investigation of industrial espionage a crew moved into a London electronics factory and installed a camera behind a one-way mirror. When two spies arrived, dressed as telephone engineers, the hidden camera recorded them bugging a telephone and photographing blueprints, thoughtfully provided by the TV company. When the crew revealed themselves, the spies told them admiringly, 'You ought to be in our business.' An unforeseen sequel was that the agency which employed the spies received a number of calls from people who wanted to hire them.

In some countries *World in Action* cameramen have posed as tourists with home movie cameras. This was done in Turkey to film people who claimed to have been tortured, and in Russia to show the extent of the dissident movement. Although 30 rolls of film were confiscated when they left Russia, they succeeded in smuggling out several 8 mm films.

When it is impossible for *World in Action* to film on location it has reconstructed events with actors. In 1964 Tim Hewat played out the Great Train Robbery on a privately owned railway line. The Post Office had refused to co-operate on details of a mail coach, but Hewat found a model makers' magazine containing scale drawings and had one built for the purpose. *World in Action* also restaged the case of an alleged Israeli spy who was kidnapped in Rome by Egyptian diplomats, drugged, strapped into a specially-fitted trunk and was in the process of being air freighted to the Middle East when he was discovered by chance. In Rome executive producer Alex Valentine bought a VW truck and had it painted in the yellow livery of the United Arab airline. He had a replica of the trunk made in the basement of his hotel and hired amateur actors to play Arab diplomats. *World in Action* drove the van from the doors of the Egyptian embassy to the airport and were filming on the tarmac before being spotted.

On another occasion actor Bill Nagy played an American Mafia boss known as Sam the Plumber in a programme based on FBI transcripts of his telephone calls, which had been bugged.

World in Action has continued to be sensational. In a 1971 stunt it persuaded 100 smokers in a Derbyshire village to give up the habit. The company placarded entrances to the village with signs reading. 'You are entering a smokeless zone', and handed out lapel badges saying 'I quit' and yo-yos for use as pacifiers. In 1975 it persuaded 390 people in a Yorkshire village to give up meat for a week in the interests of a story about making Britain self-supporting in food. Meat products were removed from the local shop and the shelves restocked with alternatives. A professor was brought in with a machine to pulp grass into food, and twice-daily meatless cookery demonstrations were provided.

In 1976 *World in Action* induced four Members of Parliament to take part in a month-long programme of physical exercise to determine whether it reduced their chances of a heart attack; and in 1984 it persuaded Conservative MP Matthew Parris to join a dole queue for a week to see how he could cope among the ranks of the unemployed. (Later he was presenter of *Weekend World*.)

Four MPs taking part in a month-long fitness experiment for World in Action *in 1976.*

A number of programmes have been banned for being too controversial. One such was an investigation into the lack of security at a radio monitoring station in Hong Kong in 1980. The programme was eventually transmitted, but in a modified form. *World in Action* executive producer Ray Fitzwalter says:

'We do not seek controversy for controversy's sake but we are not frightened of taking on things that are unpopular or difficult or may bring us up against authority. News is something that somebody doesn't want you to print. It is true that a very large part of what we transmit somebody would like to stop. Usually it makes it all the more interesting.'

Conflict

Current affairs programmes are concerned with the topical, enlarging on, or supplying background to, the news. Other forms of documentary series are not necessarily topical, if only because of the greater amount of time needed for, and allocated to, their making, but they are therefore expected to be more comprehensive.

Brian Moser was a *World in Action* producer when he got the idea for the *Disappearing World* series about the vanishing way of life of tribes threatened by the advance of 'civilisation'. He was in South America, returning through Colombia from Bolivia in 1968 after making a film about the death of guerrilla leader Che Guevara, when he came across a newspaper story. Eighteen Cuiva Indians, including eight children, had been invited to a Christmas party at a ranch where they had been shot with revolvers; their bodies had then been dumped in a pit and burned. Those responsible were land-greedy white colonists who were ruthlessly destroying the nomadic Indians. One of the men responsible for the massacre asked: 'Why not? They're just animals.'

A year later Moser returned to Colombia with a film crew and equipment including an inflatable rubber dinghy, shotguns, sheath knives, antibiotics and anti-snakebite serums, and a supply of tiny glass beads for gifts and bartering. They lived among the Indians for a year to make the first *Disappearing World* programme, shown in 1970. There was no commentator. Moser said: 'I thought to myself, why can't an Indian tell you about his life?' So the Indians told their story themselves, with subtitles. Other programmes followed, filmed in tropical forests and on mountain heights in Africa, Asia and America. The theme was the same. Moser said:

'Our aim was two-fold, to document on film various peoples and their ways of life before they disappeared, and to show the plight of minority peoples who were struggling to retain their own identity when confronted by the overbearing forces of the modern world.'

The programmes were costly in time and money. One series of six was filmed on three continents, Africa, Asia and America, with the help of anthropologists concerned with the subjects of the programmes and speaking their languages; it took two years to organise and film, but it has been seen in 93 countries.

Another great undertaking was *The World at War* in 1973, a 26-hour history of World War Two, which was more than two years in the making and cost £1 million. Nobody had ever attempted before to cover the whole war chronologically and objectively from the viewpoint of all the belligerents, for audiences that included many adults too young to remember anything of it. The story was told not just battle by battle, but with an examination of social and political developments. Juxtaposed with archive film were new interviews with commanders and politicians and also ordinary men and women who had fought and lived through the war; witnesses included Admiral Doenitz, the German U-boat commander, Marshal of the RAF Sir Arthur Harris, chief of Bomber Command, film star James Stewart who flew Liberators as a brigadier-general in the USAF, Traudl Junge, Hitler's personal secretary, and Major Otto Remer, who put down the German generals' abortive assassination of Hitler.

Producer Jeremy Isaacs (later the founding chief executive of Britain's Channel 4) was scrupulous in the use of archive film. He included only film shot at the place and time of the action it purported to show, rejecting reconstructions or scenes filmed in other years; all-purpose, any-war-any-front stock scenes of artillery barrages and street fighting were barred. His team spent tedious hours scanning old film in gloomy vaults in a large, cold castle in Coblenz and at a US Air Force base in Norton, California. Altogether five million feet of film, nearly 950 miles of it, were viewed. For one six-minute sequence in the series 85 miles of film were scanned. Some of it had never previously been shown on television. For example, there was film of the war in the Pacific shot in colour by American forces cameramen that had only recently been released.

Isaacs was wary about colour, saying that the danger was not that it made war look too horrible but that it made it look too glorious. Nevertheless, some of it shocked. The public had grown accustomed to seeing dying Asians in colour but not Europeans. Yet there were entire episodes in which no gun was fired in anger, and a programme on the Nazi attempt to exterminate all the Jews in Europe was told largely in words. Sir Laurence Olivier spoke the commentary, sometimes dramatically, but allowing moments of silence.

After years of gung-ho John Wayne and Audie Murphy movies, this was a determined attempt to tell the truth, without propaganda or editorialising. Germans were seen to stand up to British bombs as courageously as the British had to German ones, and in Britain many were surprised to discover that people in every country involved, apart from America, had experienced harder times than themselves. The series was shown in 87 countries – including West Germany and Japan.

Art, History and Ideas

Not all documentaries are objective or intended to be. They may present personal views and opinions, and one of the most celebrated was *Civilisation*, Sir Kenneth Clark's 1969 series tracing the arts which have shaped Western man. It began with Charlemagne and ended 13 programmes later among the skyscrapers of Manhattan.

The idea stemmed from the decision to let BBC 2 start colour in 1967. David Attenborough was then the channel's controller and he decided to make use of colour by putting on the screen 'the loveliest things that had been made by European man in the past thousand years'. His first move was to arrange a lunch with Sir Kenneth (later Lord) Clark, who had been Director of the

National Gallery, Chairman of the Arts Council, Chairman of the Independent Television Authority, Slade Professor of Fine Art at Oxford, and author of many art books. Sir Kenneth was intrigued by the idea and jotted down headings for a series on the back of a menu, but was reluctant to consider making it himself. He was too old, he said, and was about to start a book on Michelangelo, but later he got in touch with Attenborough and said: 'What you want is not a history of art but a whole series on the course of civilisation.' This excited him.

Sir Kenneth prepared only a broad outline. Work actually began in the middle of the series with Michelangelo, went back to the first programme, and the emergence from the Dark Ages, and returned to continuity with Voltaire. He and the team travelled 80,000 miles to make the series, his narration running to some 200,000 words, twice the size of many best-selling novels. He delivered the words urbanely, sometimes off a tele-prompter, sometimes off the cuff, in the art galleries, cathedrals and piazzas of Europe and America. He spoke in 117 locations in 11 countries and showed works from 118 museums.

'He can visualise the whole history of the world in terms of art like a movie, and give a commentary on it as compelling as Peter O'Sullevan race-reading the Derby,' said one TV critic.

Asked later what he most regretted omitting, Clark said: 'I underplayed poetry. I was so anxious to have visual sequences all the time. I ought to have done more with Shakespeare and Elizabethan England and the Book of Common Prayer.' But the series has been shown in 65 countries.

Michael Gill, who produced *Civilisation*, went on to make, in 1972, a 13-part history of the United States, Alistair Cooke's *America*, which was admired in the USA as it was in Britain. A Chicago critic confessed to 'a touch of chagrin at the uncomfortable thought that no American network or broadcaster could have put together such a programme as well'. In fact, though born in Manchester, Cooke went to America in the Thirties as a correspondent for British newspapers, and became an American citizen during World War Two. 'It was very simple,'

he said. 'I proposed to live here. My children were being born and growing up in America.'

For the series, the suave Cooke wandered across his adopted land, seeking the strands that made the present-day nation. He decided to review the American story from the first settlements, explaining later:

'The more I thought about it the more it appealed to me as a television prospect, because although I have read reams of books about America down the years, when I think of some person or episode of American history I think first of a place . . . because something charming or hideous or otherwise memorable happened there. I went over a mental map and I jotted down such places I had journeyed through, or stopped at, in many safaris across the country. . . . In all these places, and many more, something happened characteristic of the weird and wonderful effort to plant a nation across a new continent. So I put the history together from memories of the landscape and its people.'

Three years of brooding and two years of filming and writing were involved. One programme followed the trek of the early pioneers, another centred on the slave trade and the Civil War. One morning the team were in snow and hail in Arizona; that afternoon, after flying 100 miles south, they filmed in a searing hot desert.

A more surprising documentary series to become an international hit was *The Ascent of Man*, Dr Jacob Bronowski's 1974 history of scientific ideas showing, in his words: 'How man came to be drawn, step by step, from one field of scientific discovery to the next.' Bronowski, a mathematician, was born in Poland and did not learn English until he was 13, but became the National Coal Board's Director of Research, masterminding the development of smokeless fuels, and then a well-known broadcaster in radio's *Brains Trust*. He spent more than two years researching the history of science and mankind, travelling in 30 countries, to make the series, which was complex and demanding, but he proved that a good communicator can interest viewers in any subject. It has been shown in more than 60 countries.

13
Dangerous Missions
Secret Agents

John Steed and Cathy Gale got together on television in 1962, the same year that Sean Connery first introduced James Bond to cinema audiences in *Doctor No*; between them they established tongue-in-cheek secret agentry as a vogue of the decade. Steed (played by Patrick Macnee) had, in fact, made his debut as a mysterious dandyish agent in *The Avengers* two years earlier, helping Dr David Keel (Ian Hendry) in the doctor's quest to avenge the murder of his fiancée – which explains the title. However, an actors' strike halted the series and then Hendry dropped out; as the producer had several scripts left, he modified the storyline, changing the doctor's role to that of a woman, and partnering Steed with Mrs Catherine Gale, a widowed anthropologist. The new style *Avengers* was an instant success.

Whereas women previously screamed and ran when attacked in action series, Gale stood her ground. Honor Blackman, who portrayed her, said: 'I'd been used to playing women of the sweet, fair-haired English rose variety, so when the opportunity of playing Catherine Gale came my way it was like a breath of fresh air. She was a first for television – the first feminist to come into a television serial, the first woman to fight back.'

It was originally planned to equip her with a gun, but drawing it from a handbag proved clumsy, so they fitted her with a garter holster; Blackman complained that

this made her walk bow-legged and that she had to hitch up her skirt whenever she encountered an assailant. So Mrs Gale became a judo expert, hurling attackers over her shoulders. Although she had elegant clothes, including military-style suits and Chinese line dresses, these were clearly unsuitable for wearing in fights. Special clothing was required and led to her all-leather combat suits and high boots, a sensation in 1962. Blackman has recalled:

'The leather thing was extraordinary. The fact that I happened to choose leather for my fighting kit was a pure accident. Cathy led a very active life and skirts were out of the question. When your legs are flying over your head, the last thing you want to worry about is whether your stocking tops are showing. It happened that right at the beginning of the series I split my trousers in close up, so it became obvious that I had to find some tougher gear. Somebody suggested leather so I wore it throughout the rest of the show. The only things you can wear with leather trousers are boots, so they kitted me out with calf length black boots and the leather thing was born.'

To complement her gear, Steed became even more of a dandy with a style-setting penchant for braided Savile Row suits without breast pockets. He wore embroidered waistcoats and hand-made Chelsea boots, and curly brimmed bowler hats (which doubled as protective helmets). His immaculately furled umbrellas contained secret compartments that housed a swordstick, a compass and maps. Macnee said:

'I visualised Steed as a modern day Beau Brummell, and based him on a combination of Leslie Howard's Sir Percy Blakeney in *The Scarlet Pimpernel* and a performance by Ralph Richardson in a film called *Q Planes*. I considered one of the most important facets was to give him good manners. You could bash someone over the head but you always observed the social proprieties.'

While 'bashing someone over the head' was permitted, no blood was spilt in *The Avengers*. Its violence was choreographed fantasy violence. Men were killed – but never women. There was no sex either. Despite all their shared adventures, and bizarre plots which involved man-eating plants and steel robots, Steed always addressed his colleague as Mrs Gale.

In the interests of overseas sales the series was set in a picture postcard Britain with castles and stately homes, old pubs, fox hunts and cricket fields, but no concessions were made to America in the dialogue. A car was a car, not an automobile. Soon the series had an audience of 30 million in 40 countries, but not America. It was necessary to start making the programmes in colour to begin selling there in 1966, although in Britain the series was still seen in black and white. Blackman had quit by this time and been replaced by a then practically unknown Diana Rigg as Emma Peel, another widow, a wealthy woman who worked with Steed because of her love of excitement. Where Gale had used judo, Peel fought karate style, attacking villains with edge of hand, or foot. Instead of leather she wore stretch jersey catsuits and hipster pants. Some outfits were more exotic. For one episode Peel was required to disguise herself as a black-corseted Queen of Sin; this costume was too erotic for the American network censors and scenes were cut.

After two seasons Diana Rigg left to win acclaim for more serious stage acting and was replaced by Linda Thorson as Tara King, a single girl who had no martial arts skills, though she could floor villains with a punch or a swipe from her handbag. For the first time some kind of close relationship with Steed was implied, albeit discreetly; she

Diana Rigg dons martial arts gear for a karate session in The Avengers.

was the first of his partners to kiss him. The series also introduced Steed's controller, a portly, crippled man known as Mother (Patrick Newell) with an Amazonian girl assistant.

When the series came to an end in 1968 it had been seen in 70 countries. Its loss was mourned and in 1976, after the offer of financial backing from France and Canada, came *The New Avengers*, with episodes set in those countries. The problem was that Macnee was then 54 and hardly lithe. 'When you're in your fifites, however good you look or feel, you've got to act your age,' he observed. Yet, while the girls could be changed, *The Avengers* without Steed was unthinkable. The problem was solved by retaining him as a senior, more mellow, figure and leaving the action to a younger pair, Gareth Hunt as Mike Gambit, an ex-army major who had served in the Parachute Regiment and SAS, and Joanna Lumley as

Purdey (named after the guns), an ex-ballerina with close-cropped hairstyle, and an expert at Panache, fighting with straight-legged kicks and straight arm jabs. Brian Clemens said:

'To find Purdey I investigated about 700 girls, interviewed 200, read scripts with 40 and screen-tested 15. I knew Joanna Lumley was the right one. She is good to look at, witty, charming, feminine and elegant, but can knock you through a plate glass window.'

America's rival to *The Avengers* began in 1964. Ian Fleming, the creator of James Bond, had been invited to draft the outline for it and called it *Solo*; however, illness

Joanna Lumley as Purdey with side-kicks Steed and Gambit.

prevented him doing further work on it, and the makers of the Bond films objected to the proposed title because they had a character called Solo in *Goldfinger*. The new title was *The Man from U.N.C.L.E.*, an acronym that was originally meaningless. Producer Sam Rolfe said: 'People thought it stood for Uncle Sam, which it didn't, or the UN, which it didn't. Finally, so many people wanted to know what the initials stood for, we had to make up something to fit.'

That was the United Network Command

for Law Enforcement, an international agency with the responsibility for countering THRUSH, a secret organisation attempting world domination by the use of such bizarre products as ageing chemicals, will gases and vaporising machines. THRUSH, also an apparently meaningless title, was later said to stand for Technological Hierarchy for the Removal of Undesirables and the Subjugation of Humanity.

The headquarters of U.N.C.L.E. was in a dry cleaning and tailoring repair shop in New York. Agents would go into a changing cubicle in the shop, draw a curtain, and move a hook on the wall. The wall opened and they were in an office, facing a recep-

tionist who pinned triangular identity badges on them. They would then receive instructions from their British-born chief, Alexander Waverly (Leo G. Carroll), and arm themselves with Walther P38 pistols with shoulder stocks. They travelled the world – though the actors rarely left California; the world was represented by stock film scenes.

U.N.C.L.E agent Napoleon Solo (Robert Vaughn) – the name was retained from Fleming's original concept – was enigmatic, relaxed and humorous because the executive producer wanted Solo to have the light

Men from U.N.C.L.E. with their boss (David McCallum, Robert Vaughn and Leo G. Carroll).

touch that Bond possessed. Vaughn said:

'It was a part that made me an international star and which, by the time the series ended, had multiplied my annual earnings 50 times, but it destroyed my highly cherished privacy and I discovered what it was like to be the object of riots and to have to hide from strangers inside your own front door. It ran for four years and changed my life. I became a recluse, unable to go anywhere. I was tormented by fans. Teenage girls fell over my garden walls and gates, sneaked down from the hills and hid in the bushes. They climbed trees so that they could peep at me in the bath, and sent me love notes, engagement notes and proposals of marriage. I finally took refuge in a room that was not visible from the outside and would wait, hoping they would go away.'

Solo's partner was Illya Kuryakin (David McCallum), a withdrawn Slav with a blond Beatle haircut and black turtleneck sweaters. McCallum had possibly an even bigger following among fans, known as Unclies, who wore badges reading 'All the way with Illya K' and 'FLUSH THRUSH'. He has since said:

'The experience was totally shattering at the time: the complete loss of any sense of privacy and anonymity – no longer able to stroll the counters of Woolworth's unobserved. Once I tried to take a walk on Fifth Avenue in New York and they had to call out mounted police to rescue me. After a while I became completely paranoid. . . . I was the Farrah Fawcett of the Sixties. I didn't go anywhere. There were crazy scenes if I made a public appearance. On my tombstone will be "Here lies Illya Kuryakin, who was sometimes known as David McCallum".'

The first day of filming was 22 November 1963, which happened to be Robert Vaughn's birthday. He was driving to the location when on his car radio he heard the news of the shooting of President Kennedy in Dallas.

'With the exception of being told of the imminence of my mother's death, I don't think I have ever had a comparable shock. Oddly enough, the plot of the U.N.C.L.E. introductory story which I had to begin filming that day was about the threatened assassination of the President of a Latin American country.'

Four years later the series was showing in 62 countries, and had spawned a spin-off, *The Girl from U.N.C.L.E.*, with agents April Dancer (Stefanie Powers) and Mark Slate (Noel Harrison, son of Rex). British Unclies were as hysterical as their American counterparts, as Vaughn discovered when he visited London (after stopping on the way for a weekend with Robert Kennedy's family in Virginia because the Senator's children wanted to meet the star).

'I arrived at Heathrow airport at about 9 pm, and as I was preparing to go through Customs I heard an extraordinary chant growing in volume: "So-lo, So-lo, So-lo . . ." It was frightening. I was with my bodyguard, but as we left the Customs area we were overwhelmed. Thousands of teenagers grabbed at me, ripped my clothes, and actually raised me off the ground. I had to hide in a lavatory until the police could clear a way to my car. It was the kind of experience that I thought only pop singers endured, but for several years it was a regular occurrence wherever I travelled in Asia or Europe.'

The Man from U.N.C.L.E. ended in 1968, the same year as *The Avengers*, although the stars were reunited in a TV movie *The Return of the Man from U.N.C.L.E.* in 1983, by which time Leo G. Carroll was long dead, and the Waverly part was played by Patrick Macnee.

Agents Galore

Rival agent shows of varying degrees of seriousness multiplied in the Sixties. *I Spy* in 1965 had American undercover agents Kelly Robinson (Robert Culp) and Alexander Scott (Bill Cosby) travelling the world, masquerading respectively as an international tennis player and his multilingual trainer. In the same year *Get Smart*, an out and out spoof created by Mel Brooks and Buck Henry, had Maxwell Smart (Don Adams) as the bumbling, incompetent agent 86 of C.O.N.T.R.O.L., an international agency with headquarters in a music hall, waging war against an evil organisation known as K.A.O.S. 'Sorry about that, Chief,'

A new generation emerges from the destruction in Winds of War.

Overleaf Wealthy Kate Browning (Lee Remick) *has marital designs on* Mistral (Stacey Keach) *in* Mistral's Daughter.

Patrick Swayze and Lesley-Anne Down as Southern gentleman and Creole belle in North and South.

*Always the bridesmaid
. . . Mavis Riley wishes
happiness to Len and
Rita Fairclough.*

*Elton John, one of many
celebrities who braved
being upstaged on* the
Muppet Show.

Spitting Image *has offended many viewers by guying the Queen and Prince Charles.*

The subject is golf, but Benny Hill can find broad humour in any topic.

was Smart's refrain. His cover was as a greetings card salesman and his equipment included a telephone in one of his shoes, though it rarely worked. He was helped by Agent 99 (Barbara Feldon) and Agent K13, a dog named Fang.

Mission Impossible, a year later, featured the Impossible Missions Force, a secret American government organisation handling sensitive international assignments such as training a cat to carry out a burglary. Each of the agents was an expert in a specialised field. For example, Rollin Hand was a master of disguise. Martin Landau, who played him, was sometimes called on to adopt five different disguises in an episode, and said:

'Make-up for some of these take as long as two hours, and are so expert that people who know me will walk past me without noticing the make up. Once when I was playing the part of a crotchety old man only the wardrobe master recognised me – by the costume.'

Landau's wife, Barbara Bain, played Cin-

The Champions had extraordinary powers, but not, apparently, over the weather . . .

namon Carter whose speciality, for fairly obvious reasons, was distraction, although the pair were later replaced by Paris (Leonard Nimoy) and Dana (Lesley Ann Warren). The head of the unit was Jim Phelps (Peter Graves) and each episode began with him entering a building and finding a hidden parcel containing a tape recording. The voice on the tape (that of actor Bob Johnson) declared: 'Your mission, Jim, should you decide to accept it, is . . . [*details followed*] As usual, should you or any member of your IM Force be captured or killed, the Secretary will disavow any knowledge of your existence. This tape will self-destruct in five seconds.'

When the time elapsed the tape and recorder would erupt in smoke.

The Champions, in 1967, were members of a small, secret agency based in Geneva and known by the code name Nemesis. It had been formed by the nations of the world to combat any situation that could result in international tension or warfare. It was supported by all countries but answerable to none.

Its trio of agents – an American, Craig Stirling (Stuart Damon) and two Britons, Sharron Macready (Alexandra Bastedo) and Richard Barrett (William Gaunt) – possessed remarkable powers acquired after a plane crash in Tibet. Mysterious rescuers not only healed them but heightened the efficiency of their bodies, minds and senses so that, in action, they could call on acute sight, smell and hearing, highly developed extra-sensory perception, telepathy, reasoning powers and understanding of mathematical formulae. Their uncanny powers were a secret and a bond between them. However, they could make mistakes and could be killed. Producer Monty Berman explained:

'Our aim is to make incredibility credible. Action dramas have reached the stage when the principal characters are achieving the impossible in their exploits. One man can defeat a dozen several times in the course of a single story. No one can believe that any mortal could achieve what the present day heroes manage to do and survive, but *The Champions* makes it all logical because the three characters have these out of the ordinary powers. They can't perform miracles because they are not superhuman, but they can do anything within the limits of human capabilities. Whatever they do in the stories, someone in the world is capable of doing the same. They simply have all these abilities rolled into one. But they can't do anything that some other human being hasn't achieved somewhere, sometime, and they are vulnerable because they can never know just how far they can go without exceeding the limits of human ability.'

The Riddle of the Prisoner

The most remarkable secret agent series of the Sixties or any other era was Patrick McGoohan's compulsive but puzzling *The Prisoner*. From 1959 to 1962 McGoohan had played John Drake, a laconic, globe-trotting special security agent in *Danger Man*. Almost every week he was seen in a different country – though these 'world settings', as the publicity material called

them, were achieved with stock film sequences. It was seen in almost every part of the world and there was wide curiosity about what McGoohan would do next. McGoohan's answer in 1967 was *The Prisoner*, about a former secret agent captured and brainwashed in a curious village from which there was no escape. Sir Lew Grade bought the idea on the strength of a few outline pages and gave McGoohan *carte blanche*.

It opened in London with a jet of vapour hissing through a keyhole. The occupant of the room clutched at his throat, staggered, fell and passed out. When he regained consciousness he lurched to a window for air, but the scene outside was unfamiliar. The buildings suggested Italy but everything else refuted this. (The series was, in fact, filmed in Portmeirion, the extraordinary Italianate village in North Wales designed by architect Sir Clough Williams-Ellis.) There were shops, cafes, a hotel and a village square. People in the streets wore straw hats and blazers or multi-coloured capes as though dressed for a carnival, and open taxis had colourful awnings.

The place was known simply as 'the Village' and although it looked like a holiday camp it was a prison camp, isolated by mountains, forests and sea. The Prisoner had a cottage with maid service and all amenities, but it was bugged, and his every move was watched on close-circuit television. Detailed maps of the village were obtainable in shops but they marked features simply as 'the Mountains' and 'the Sea', without names, and while there were exits from the village a deadly ray barrier made them impassable. There was also Rover, a terrifying plastic balloon which would bound after and shrink-wrap an escapee.

The reason for the Prisoner's captivity was as much a mystery as where he was being held. His identity was not disclosed. (He was not John Drake, said McGoohan emphatically.) He was a man who had held a highly secret job, had quit, but still knew secrets which many people, friends or enemies, would like to discover. He did not know who had abducted him. They could be his own former colleagues, they could be enemies, perhaps both; they could be from the East, trying to break him, or from the

West, training him to resist indoctrination and seeing how much he could take.

The man behind the organisation was referred to as Number One, but never seen. The Prisoner's direct contact was Number Two, but there was a new Number Two every time the Prisoner encountered him. The Prisoner himself was addressed as Number Six – which he refused to acknowledge. 'I'm not a number, I'm a free man,' he roared defiantly.

He had no idea who the other prisoners were. All had been associated with highly confidential jobs for one country or another. Some had been brainwashed in the Village's conditioning centre, known as the Castle, and had accepted their new life. Others fought on for survival as individuals. *The Prisoner* remained a series of mysteries to the end. It involved nightmarish cat-and-mouse games of spirit-sapping tortures, subtle, scientific brainwashing and malignant mind-probing, through all of which the Prisoner continued with abortive escape bids.

This was Patrick McGoohan's series. He devised it, was executive producer and starred in it. He had a hand in writing every script and directed a number of episodes. Never before had one man taken so much responsibility for a series. Before it began he said: 'If people don't like it, there's only one person to blame – me!'

People liked it. They were also bewildered and irritated by its timeless gadgetry and strange, convoluted plots, by its gimmicky switching of characters playing the oppressive Number Two, and by its secret symbols which included an old penny-farthing bicycle and a mute, midget butler, who often carried an open umbrella. I sought answers from McGoohan when he was cutting the final episode. 'I've done a job,' he snapped. 'I set out to make a specific number of films. I've made them. The series has come to an end. It's just the end of a job, that's all.' Taxed with the absence of continuity between episodes, the lack of logical progression in his captors' extraordinary attempts to break the Prisoner, and in his escape bids, he demanded: 'Do you find life always logical?'

He refused to consider making more episodes. He never even returned to Port-meirion. *The Prisoner* always had its fans and re-runs turned it into a cult with an appreciation society called Six of One which continues to hold an annual convention, its members wearing blazers and multicoloured capes like the inhabitants of the Village.

Agents of the Seventies

The procession of agent shows on the screen continued in the Seventies with *Department S* which concerned a special investigation branch of Interpol, based in Paris, undertaking to solve crimes for any law enforcement agency in the world. Its unlikely operatives, whose cases were assigned them by Sir Curtis Seretse (Dennis Alaba Peters), an African attached to the United Nations, were Jason King (Peter Wyngarde), a crime novelist, Annabelle Hurst (Rosemary Nichols), a computer programmer, and American Stewart Sullivan (Joel Fabiani), whose talents seemed to be in his knuckles.

The character of the flamboyant novelist, whose technique in handling cases was to ask himself what his detective hero would do, emerged as the dominant one, and a subsequent series was called simply *Jason King*. In this he was still a wealthy, pleasure-loving writer seeking backgrounds for his best-selling Mark Caine novels, but was no longer attached to Department S, and was free to roam the world. In Australia 30,000 women reportedly voted Wyngarde the man they would most like to be seduced by.

The Six Million Dollar Man, in 1973, was based on Martin Caidin's book *Cyborg* and brought the word 'bionic' (meaning a person operated electronically) into popular use. The hero, Steve Austin (Lee Majors) was an astronaut and NASA pilot before a crash on a test flight left him all but dead, with much of his body destroyed. He was reconstructed by advanced medical technology, his legs, one arm and one eye being replaced at a cost of six million dollars with synthetic, nuclear-powered mechanisms which made him a cyborg (cybernetic organism), part human, part machine, with extraordinary powers. He could break chains, rip open doors, batter his way through walls and run at 60 mph, which gave him considerable advantages over adversaries. Nevertheless, he was not a robot and remained vulnerable.

Bionic hero Steve Austin (Lee Majors) in The Six Million Dollar Man.

Damage to his limbs could be repaired but if he was shot in a vital organ he would die.

He employed his bionic limbs on behalf of the OSO (Office of Strategic Operations), later the OSI (Office of Scientific Intelligence), an organisation like the CIA, international in scope, where a fellow agent and girlfriend was Jaime Sommers (Lindsay Wagner), who was similarly rebuilt after being critically injured in a sky-diving accident. She was later the heroine of a spin-off series, *The Bionic Woman*, which also introduced Bionic Boy (played by Vincent Van Patten) and Bionic Dog. 'Bionic' became an overworked adjective in newspapers for anyone possessed of great strength or endurance.

The Professionals was created in 1978 by Brian Clemens, who was also behind *The Avengers*. However, this was no tongue-in-cheek fantasy but a taut, slick, thriller series with shootings, bomb blasts, fires, and chases by car and boat, criticised by some for its violence. One episode involved a close copy of the 1980 SAS raid on the Iranian Embassy in London.

Gordon Jackson cast off his image as Hudson, the butler in *Upstairs, Downstairs*, to play George Cowley, the demanding boss of an organisation known as CI5, his chief agents being the ruthless Bodie and his slightly more sensitive partner, Doyle (Lewis Collins and Martin Shaw), who had no compunction about shooting to kill. Shaw and Collins became macho sex symbols but paid a price in injuries. Their medical records included three broken ankles (Shaw 2, Collins, 1), three concussions (Collins 2, Shaw 1), one broken collarbone (Collins), and 27 stitches (Collins 5, Shaw 22). 'We have always encouraged Martin and Lewis to do their own stunts unless it is positively dangerous,' said Clemens.

14
Simply
Fantastic

Science Fiction

The most enduring character in television science fiction has been *Dr Who*, the eccentric scientist-adventurer travelling the planets and the centuries past, present and future in his time machine, a converted police box known as the Tardis (an acronym for Time and Relative Dimension in Space) – and usually landing, for various reasons, in an unintended place or age. He was first played in 1963 by William Hartnell, and since then the role has been played on television by six more actors: Patrick Troughton, Jon Pertwee, Tom Baker, Peter Davison, Colin Baker and Sylvester McCoy. They were different in appearance and adopted different characteristics but this was explained in the story by the fact that the Doctor was not from Earth,

Five Doctors: Pertwee (at wheel), Baker, Davison, Troughton and Hurndall (as Hartnell).

being a 750-year-old time lord with two hearts. A programme called *The Five Doctors* in 1983 brought together three veteran Doctors in person, two others on old film clips, plus another actor, Richard Hurndall, impersonating the first Doctor.

The title came from an occasion when he was addressed as 'Dr Foreman' because he happened to be standing in a yard beneath a signboard bearing that surname. 'Dr *Who*?' he snapped, and he has been Dr Who ever since. Budgets have always been relatively modest, that for the pilot programme, transmitted on the day after President Kennedy's assassination, being a mere £2,000. The success of *Dr Who* has been largely due to the fanciful creatures against which he and his various youthful travelling companions have been pitted. Ice Warriors, Cybermen, Yetis and Drashigs have menaced him; there have also been the less well-remembered Gundans, Urbankans, Ograms, Mechanoids, Plasmatons and Terileptils, but the most popular have been the Daleks, gliding, swivelling pepper pots which reiterate

'Exterminate! Exterminate!' grate the Daleks as they menace Doctor Who (Jon Pertwee).

mechanically, 'Exterminate, exterminate!' Parents, many of whom watched as children, and still watch avidly, have complained that sometimes the monsters have been too horrifying and their children have been forced to look away from the screen, but Terry Nation, the writer who created the Daleks, claims: 'The answer is simple: kids love to be frightened.'

More than 75 books of Doctor adventures have been published, and there are fan clubs in many countries including America, where the series acquired cult status in the Seventies, and conventions have been attended by fans wearing over-long woollen scarves like those of the Doctor.

Monsters also figured in the American series, *Voyage to the Bottom of the Sea*, which was set two decades in the future when made in 1964, though its future is now the past. It was produced, directed and written by Irwin Allen and stemmed from a movie of the same title which he wrote in 1961 about a submarine of the future saving the world from incineration. As all the sets and props and thousands of feet of underwater film were available for further use, he went on to make 110 episodes for television.

Generally referred to as 'the tin fish', *Seaview* was a 600 ft-long nuclear-powered research submarine based, for security reasons, in a pen 200 ft below the sea at the Nelson Institute of Marine Research, a private scientific bureau directed by Admiral Harriman Nelson (Richard Basehart). It had a glass-nosed observation room, torpedo compartments for atomic missiles, and a speed of 70 knots. In fact there were five *Seaviews*, ranging from an 18 ft model, used for surface shots, to a 4 ft miniature, and Bill Abbott, the special effects supervisor, won two Emmy Awards for them.

Seaview's main activity was to defend the human race against mad scientists and creatures which included beings from other worlds, replica humans, humanoid amphibians, dinosaurs, giant jellyfish and werewolves. One episode took place inside a whale, for which a tubular set was built and lined with vinyl bags which were inflated and deflated to simulate breathing, while it was lit by red and yellow lights.

Into Space

Irwin Allen went on in 1965 to create, produce, write and direct *Lost in Space*, which he had the foresight to set further ahead – in the year 1997, after the world's population explosion had prompted an exploratory colonising voyage into space. The destination chosen as being best for human survival was a planet circling Alpha Centauri. Members of the expedition, chosen from millions of volunteers, were astrophysicist John Robinson (Guy Williams), his biochemist wife Maureen (June Lockhart) and their three children, and Major Donald West (Mark Goddard) their geologist-pilot. They were also accompanied by a robot, a 7 ft-tall bundle of bolts and nuts which could wash, trim and set the explorers' hair, launder, compute tax returns, dance, recite poetry, play chess and the guitar, and solve crossword puzzles in split seconds.

They entered their spacecraft, Jupiter 2, in silver space suits and were placed in suspended animation in individual plastic tubes, expecting to wake up 98 years later in a new world, but Col. Zachary Smith (Jonathan Harris), a spy, crept on board and reprogrammed the robot to destroy the mission. However, through miscalculating the countdown he became a reluctant stowaway, and his excess weight and the deranged robot caused severe damage to the navigational guidance system. The astronauts, thawed out by Smith after crash-landing on an unknown planet, found themselves out of communication with the rest of the universe, having no idea of the year or what galaxy they were in. Their only friend was a creature they discovered – a cross between a puppy, a monkey and a teddy bear – which became a pet they called 'the Bloop'. The scenes were actually filmed in the Mojave desert, east of Hollywood.

All these shows were meant primarily for youngsters. The first seriously-intentioned sci-fi series with continuing characters, intended for adults and based on contemporary scientific research (with help from NASA), was *Star Trek*, in 1966. It was set 200 years in the future on a space ship patrolling the universe, and encountering monsters and mysteries everywhere. The much-quoted, infinitive-splitting introduction to each programme ran:

'Space, the final frontier. These are the voyages of the Starship *Enterprise*. Its five year mission: to explore new worlds, to seek out new life and new civilisations, to boldly go where no man has gone before.'

As conceived by Gene Roddenberry, who had written for *Highway Patrol*, *Naked City* and *Dr Kildare*, the *Enterprise* (originally to be called the *Yorktown*), was the largest starship in the fleet of the United Federation of Planets, bigger than a battleship and with a crew of 430 on eight decks. (The models used for filming were actually 12 ft and 2 ft long.) It was faster than light, capable of 700 million mph, though speed was expressed in warp factors, warp 1 being the speed of light. It could cruise at warp 6 (or 216 times the speed of light) and had a top speed of warp 8 (or 512 times the speed of light) but that put it under stress. For defence the ship had sensor deflector shields (an invisible force barrier), phasers (which emitted beams of pulsating energy) and photon torpedoes.

The starship never landed (which saved production costs). Instead, its officers were 'beamed down' in *Star Trek*'s most famous effect. A device in the circular transporter room could convert matter into energy, transmit it to any point up to 16,000 miles away and reconstitute it in its original form. So, 'Beam us down, Scotty,' they would order the Engineering Officer and would dematerialise to reappear on land. Aluminium dust was scattered through a beam of high intensity light to create the dissolving effect.

For defence on their walkabouts the crew carried portable phasers, the beams from which could stun or dematerialise any molecular form. The smallest was worn on a belt beneath the pocketless velour uniform shirt; a larger model had a pistol mount holding a power pack. Their principal enemies were the Romulans, a militaristic race with an organisation like that of the Roman empire, though with complete equality between the sexes. The Romulans' allies were the murderous, completely untrustworthy Klingons, who treated women like animals, but there were other hostile peoples and environments. On one planet the explorers aged to 90.

Canadian actor William Shatner played the American commanding officer, Capt. James T. Kirk (whose name was originally going to be Robert T. April). Leonard Nimoy played Mr Spock, the first officer, half-Earthling, half-Vulcan, with pointed ears (which Nimoy found painful to wear), green blood and a logical mind. He suppressed all emotions, was telepathic and had total recall. He could render an enemy helpless with a pinch on the neck. The network was originally unhappy about Spock, fearing he might repel viewers; instead he became the favourite character. DeForest Kelley played Dr Leonard (Bones) McCoy, the testy, unmilitary, American chief medical officer with whom Spock bickered. Other regulars were Engineering Officer Montgomery Scott (James Doohan), a Scot, Helmsman Sulu (George Takei), who was of Japanese descent, Ensign Chekov, the Russian navigator (Walter Koenig) and Communications Officer Uhura (Nichelle Nichols), an African. The network also worried about this integrated crew, fearing it might cause offence; it did not.

Star Trek was slow to win popularity. After 78 episodes production was ended in 1969, the year it began to succeed, and coincidentally the year man walked on the moon. Termination brought a million letters of complaint, leading to re-runs which were more popular than the first screenings. One American station went on to screen an episode daily for ten years. More than 400 clubs were set up for Trekkies, as the fans called themselves – one of them exclusively for grandmothers – and they have continued to hold conventions, wearing costumes identifying themselves as crew members. America's first reusable orbiting vehicle, the space shuttle, was named the *Enterprise* by President Gerald Ford in honour of the series.

Cartoon episodes were made with the voices of the TV cast; then, ten years after the last episode, *Star Trek: the Motion Picture*, followed by other films. Finally, in 1988, came *Star Trek: the Next Generation*, another 22 episodes for television, though Roddenberry had changed the cast. Capt. Kirk was replaced by a Frenchman, Capt. Jean-Luc Picard (played by British actor Patrick Stewart), who commanded a new starship eight times larger than the old one, and carrying 1,000 people, including families.

Space 1999 was a British-made *Star Trek* in 1975, about a space station driven out of orbit around the moon and travelling through the universe. It was made by Gerry and Sylvia Anderson, who had moved on from *Thunderbirds* and other puppet series to employing human actors, but who still utilised their expertise at special effects, model-making and table top photography. They had already made one science fiction series, *UFO*, in 1970, which was set in the near future – the 1980s – with a cast that included Ed Bishop as commander of SHADO (Supreme Headquarters, Alien Defence Organisation), an organisation set up to defend Earth against unidentified flying objects, with interceptor craft crewed by girls in flesh-tinted, skin-tight cat suits and

Commander Adama (Lorne Greene) in the control centre of Battlestar Galactica.

mauve wigs, controlled from a base on the moon.

Space 1999 was set in 1999 when man was using the dark side of the moon as a dump for nuclear waste. The waste exploded, tearing the moon apart and hurling Moonbase Alpha, which had been monitoring the dumping, out of orbit and into space with 300 people on board. The stars were the craft's Commander Koenig (Martin Landau), and two of his officers, Prof. Victor Bergman (Barry Morse) and Dr Helena Russell (Barbara Bain). Joan Collins also appeared – in silver, green and mauve eye shadow – as Kara, Director of Reconstruction on the ship. The crew wore unisex garments with different coloured sleeves to indicate their departments.

Some of their experiences were closely akin to those of *Star Trek*'s officers. One episode featured a planet where all feelings were reversed, the inhabitants laughing when in pain and crying when happy. Another planet had Arctic wastes (made from solidified fire extinguisher foam) where Ice Maidens inappropriately favoured revealing cleavage.

After the first year Gerry and Sylvia Anderson split up matrimonially and professionally, and Anderson brought in Fred Freiberger who had produced the third season of *Star Trek*. New characters included an alien, Maya (Catherine Schell), a sort of female Spock, capable of transforming herself into any form of organic matter – such as a tree, a gorilla or a lion. (A cage was built for the camera crew, so that animals could roam the set.) A co-production with the Italian television organisation, RAI, *Space 1999* was dubbed into Italian, French and German, and although it was not even fully networked on ITV in Britain, Sir Lew Grade managed to sell it around the world.

Battlestar Galactica (1978) concerned a greater disaster. It was the story of the last members of the human race fleeing from destruction by powerful metallic creatures called Cylons. The twelve colonies of man had been blown to radioactive dust, but ancient writings told of a thirteenth colony in another galaxy with a similar life form. Its name was Earth, and reaching it was their only hope of survival. *Galactica*, a space ship more than a mile long, with a cruising speed measured in light seconds, led the way, trailed by an incredible convoy of airbuses, rocket-powered taxis, interplanetary tramp steamers and commuter space shuttles. Executive producer Glen A. Larson said the series had no time-frame:

'The exodus in space could be happening now or a million years from now. Or perhaps these people reached Earth a long time ago and became our ancestors. In terms of the architecture of the time the Pyramids shouldn't exist, but they do. So who built them? Who designed the fantastic highways off the island of Bimini, leading into the sea? Why is it that so many different cultures share the same legends, like the lost city of Atlantis? Our story hints at one possible answer.'

Galactica itself was a city in space, ten times larger than a present-day aircraft carrier, its bridge an electronic control centre equipped with computers which could launch turbo-thrusters to strike back at the bat-winged Cylon warships. Miles from the studio a special effects team built a scale model of the *Galactica* with thousands of working parts, flickering lights and suspended pods from which jet fighters would appear to zoom into battle. Photographed by a manoeuvrable camera on narrow gauge tracks, it could make a stationary object seem to soar, spin, loop or dive. All this, and a big cast that included Lorne Greene as Commander Adama, Richard Hatch as his son, Capt. Apollo, and Dirk Benedict as Lt. Starbuck, a fighter pilot, helped to make the series one of the most expensive ever made.

The interstellar refugees were garbed in styles suggested by ancient Egyptian and Greek mythology. The Cylon warriors, who acknowledged their leaders' commands with 'By your leave', were encased in gleaming chrome, except for eye-level apertures through which a narrow beam of red light pulsated. (They were difficult to film because the chrome reflected every light on the set but the effect was too intriguing to abandon.)

The series had its own glossary. *Scare the pogees out of* meant to frighten. *Cut through the feldegar* meant eliminate the bull. *Frack* was an expletive. A *cubit* was a gold coin, a *fumarello*, a cigar, *hydronic mushies*, tasty health food.

Some critics saw the series as *Wagon Train* in space, with the Cylons as the Red Indians. Larson replied that his inspiration was the biblical episode of Moses leading the Hebrew fugitives across the Red Sea, and that the Cylons were the Egyptian army.

Invasion of Earth

There was no doubt about the source of inspiration for *The Invaders* in 1966; it was a variation on *The Fugitive*, the series about a doctor on the run from the law, which was reaching its climax at this time (see Chapter 16). It was made by the same team, but it concerned an architect on the run from alien invaders from a doomed planet, who were using their ability to assume human form to infiltrate society with the intention of gaining control of Earth. Not surprisingly, he was unable to get anyone to believe him. The producer trailed it like this:

'They're here among us now . . . in your city . . . maybe on your block. They're invaders . . . alien beings from another planet — but they look just like us. Take a look around — casually. No sense letting them know you're suspicious. The new neighbours across the street. . . the substitute teacher, that too-pretty secretary in your husband's office . . . anyone of them might be an invader from outer space. How can you tell? Sometimes their hands are mutilated, the little finger jutting out awkwardly. Sometimes, rarely, they will begin to glow, when they are in need of regeneration in order to retain their human form, and always they are without a pulse or a heartbeat, for, of course, they possess no hearts.'

In the first episode David Vincent (Roy Thinnes) was driving on a deserted country road when he saw a flying saucer land. On his return to the scene with police, they found only a young couple who denied seeing anything strange. The police dismissed Vincent's story, but he noticed that the pair had crooked little fingers. From then on Vincent was on the run from the aliens, and was beaten, almost burned to death in a hotel room and held in a psychiatric ward.

Frustratingly for fans, it ended after 43 episodes without any kind of conclusion.

More repellent aliens invaded Los Angeles in *V* in 1983. They were creatures from the constellation of Sirius, similar in appearance to humans, except that when their skin was torn it revealed a lizard-like skin beneath. They arrived in a fleet of 31 giant saucers, each three to five miles wide, ostensibly on a peace mission, offering their advanced scientific and medical knowledge in exchange for aid in making a chemical compound necessary to their existence. In fact they were after food – consisting of humans whom they stored in tanks on the ships.

When the true intentions of 'the Visitors', as they were known, were discovered, a Resistance movement was formed, using the V for Victory sign that was chalked on buildings as a symbol of defiance in Nazi-occupied countries during World War Two. The story had many parallels with that war. The invaders represented the Nazis, their Shock Troopers the SS, and their unseen leader, back in Sirius, the Führer. They had a propaganda machine, youth cadres and informers, and there were Jews in the Resistance.

The series required an elaborate set, built on stages 25 and 26 at the Burbank studios in California. There sat the mother ship and five movable spaceships, including the Supreme Commander's, and its squadron of four fighters, ranging from 18 ft to 68 ft in length, which could be moved to different locations by tractors. All the ships were composed of modules so that each could fulfil different functions; full-size they were passenger vehicles or giant tankers, but the front and rear pieces alone served as fighter craft. Inside the mother ship was a master control room with dozens of computer and television screens and consoles equipped with blinking lights, buttons and switches, the living quarters of Diana (the Visitors' second-in-command), and long, labyrinthine corridors with walls that lit up.

Some of the actors who played Visitors had wearying sessions in the make-up department, because their faces had to be covered with masks of foam latex so that what appeared to be human skin could be ripped off to reveal lizard skin underneath.

Diana (Jane Badler), leader of the reptilian invaders in V, *munches a mouse.*

It took close on three hours to transform actress Jane Badler into Diana, and it took longer to devise a method by which she could be seen to swallow a live guinea-pig. Diana had to open her mouth a full six inches, which was humanly impossible for the actress; so make-up supervisor Leo Lotito and his team designed a mechanical head with a hinged mouth that could be opened to that extent by hydraulic rams. A mask with skin and fibre gills was then made to fit on the mechanical head. When the scene was filmed, Badler lifted the rodent to her mouth, at which point the cameras cut to the dummy, and Badler dropped the animal in its mouth.

In another scene in *V*, a scientist's daughter gave birth to twins after falling for a Visitor. One looked human, apart from having a reptilian forked tongue. The other baby was a lizard. *V* was a series that shocked.

15
Pow, Bam and Splatt!

Superheroes from Comic Strips

In a city street people stared upwards. 'It's a bird! It's a plane! It's Superman!' they chorused. An announcer spoke:

'Yes, it's Superman, strange visitor from another planet, who came to Earth with powers and abilities far beyond those of mortal men . . . Superman, who can change the course of mighty rivers, bend steel in his bare hands and who – disguised as Clark Kent, mild-mannered reporter for a great metropolitan newspaper – fights a never ending battle for truth, justice and the American way.'

That was the regular opening of *The Adventures of Superman*, which began in 1953, starring the superhero from the planet Krypton, created in 1938 by writer Jerome Siegel and artist Joe Shuster, and featured in comic books and strips in 250 newspapers, as well as on radio and in movie serials.

Television could not then run to the lavish disaster scenes of the *Superman* films of the Seventies and Eighties, so the action consisted largely of rescuing his newspaper colleagues, Lois Lane (Phyllis Coates) and Jimmy Olsen (Jack Larson) from kidnapping and other dangers. Superman himself was played by 6 ft 2½ in-tall George Reeves, a useful light heavyweight boxer, though the muscles that bulged what he called his 'monkey suit' were bolstered with foam rubber. Reeves beat more than 200 aspirants for the role, but came to regret it because he was typecast. His appearance in a minor part in *From Here to Eternity* was greeted with yells by a preview audience, after which his part was cut, and with other roles unobtainable he was forced to work as a wrestler. When he shot himself in 1959 his fiancée said he had taken his life because 'he was known as Superman to nine million children but couldn't get a job'.

Superman was one of the first of many superheroes who transferred from comic strips to television. *Batman*, in 1966, was based on a strip by Bob Kane, first seen in 1939 in a comic, and a film serial in the Forties: the caped crusader saving Gotham City from the likes of the Joker and the Penguin.

Batman and Robin (otherwise wealthy Bruce Wayne and his 15-year-old ward, Dick Grayson) lived in a grand house, Wayne Manor, but when they got calls for help on the Batphone, they headed for a secret door behind a bookcase in the den and slid down Batpoles to the Batcave. After a quick change into their Batgear they would be pursuing crooks in their Batmobile. This was a converted Lincoln, 17 ft long and weighing two and a half tons, with windshield bubbles made of aircraft glass, and with six-inch flared steel tyre protectors. Batman and Robin set an example by always fastening seat belts before a chase. The only person who knew their secret was Alfred, the butler (Alan Napier).

Robin was given to sycophantic congratulations such as, 'Quick thinking, Batman!'

A bird? A plane? No, the shape beneath the wrinkled wool is Superman *George Reeves.*

and to extraordinary exclamations such as 'Holy fork in the road' and 'Holy hole in a doughnut'. The oddest were 'Holy contributing to the delinquency of minors' and 'Holy priceless collection of Etruscan snoods'. Sometimes they were joined by Batgirl, otherwise librarian Barbara Gordon (Yvonne Craig), daughter of the Police Commissioner. She rode a Batcycle.

The TV series came about after a network employed market researchers to establish the five favourite comic book characters with a view to making a series. They were – in order of popularity – Dick Tracy, Super-man, Batman, the Green Hornet and Little Orphan Annie. Rights to the first two were unobtainable, so Batman was the choice. It was the first television show to be camped up deliberately for laughs. Executive producer William Dozier admitted:

'I had never heard of Batman. I had never even seen a comic book. I bought a dozen comic books and felt like a fool doing it. I read them and asked myself, what could I do with *this*? I decided to exaggerate seriousness

— to make the show so serious that it was funny. I think the mood of the country was just ready for something wild and crazy.'

First choice for the title role was Ty Hardin, but he was unavailable, and it went to Adam West who had played minor roles in *The Detectives*. That of Robin went to Burt Ward who was 20 but looked younger. He had no previous acting experience but was a karate expert.

Every episode ended with a cliffhanger, with Batman and Robin in an impossible

Adam West as Batman, *the camp crusader recognisable by bat cape, bat hood and bat suit.*

plight, from which they escaped swiftly at the start of the next. It parodied every TV and comic book cliché and the dialogue was stilted to match the balloons of comic strips. Exclamations and onomatopoeic sound effects were superimposed as captions: CRASH!, CRUNCH!, KLONK!, ZAP!, WHAMM!, AARGH!, OOF!, POWIE!, SPLATT!

126

Some of the humour was delicious. In the first episode Batman went into a disco, wearing cowl, cape and tights, but refused the offer of a stageside seat, explaining: 'No, thank you, I don't want to be conspicuous.' He then walked to the bar and ordered an orange juice.

That first episode had Frank Gorshin as the Riddler, in long johns embroidered with question marks, and Jill St John as his moll, after which stars queued for villainous roles. They included Tallulah Bankhead as the Black Widow, Anne Baxter as Zelda the Great, Art Carney as the Archer, Joan Collins as the Siren, Zsa Zsa Gabor as Minerva, Glynis Johns as Lady Peasoup, Van Johnson as the Minstrel, Eartha Kitt as the Catwoman, Roddy McDowall as the Bookworm, Burgess Meredith as the Penguin, Ethel Merman as Lola Lasagna, Otto Preminger as Mr Freeze, Vincent Price as the Egghead, Cesar Romero as the Joker, Pierre Salinger as Lucky Pierre, and Shelley Winters as Ma Parker. Other famous stars were glimpsed fleetingly – sometimes peering from a window as Batman scaled a building. Among them were Frank Sinatra, Sammy Davis Jr and Edward G. Robinson.

The series brought Batmania. Youngsters wore Batmasks, went to bed in Batjamas, and drove miniature Batmobiles. Teenage girls had Batcuts, in which the hairline was shaped to imitate Batman's cowl.

Dozier also produced in the same year *The Green Hornet*, featuring another masked hero of the comic strips, although his other clothes were more conventional. The Hornet (played by Van Williams) was newspaper editor Britt Reid, allegedly the great-grandson of the Lone Ranger. He also had a supercar, Black Beauty, and the Hornet Sting, which used high pitched sound to knock people unconscious or flatten doors. The Green Hornet, however, was less successful, despite Kato, the Hornet's Oriental chauffeur and kung-fu expert, being played by Bruce Lee.

Big Man, Big Girl

Tarzan first appeared in a book by Edgar Rice Burroughs in 1914, and later in many films, but he had also featured extensively in comic strips. The man who preferred life in the jungle, where he had been orphaned as a baby, to life as Lord Greystoke in England, was played on television from 1966 by Ron Ely. There was no Jane in the series; his friend in the jungle was a chimp, Cheetah. It was an expensive series made in Brazil and Mexico, the production beset by rains and stomach troubles and taking three or four times as long to shoot as it would have in a studio. Ely was called on to ride a zebra bareback, to wrestle a lion, and frequently to swing from vine to vine. On one occasion he lost his hold and fell 28 ft; the scene remained in, though the fall was explained by having Tarzan shot.

Wonder Woman was a comic strip original invented by Charles Moulton in 1941. When it transferred to television in 1976 the role was played by 6 ft-tall Lynda Carter, who had been Miss USA three years earlier.

The girl in the star-spangled-knickers, Wonder Woman *Lynda Carter.*

Wonder Woman was, in fact, Princess Diana, daughter of Queen Hippolyte of the Amazons, whose home was on uncharted Paradise Island somewhere in the Bermuda Triangle. During World War Two an American fighter pilot, Steve Trevor (Lyle Waggoner), crashed on the island and Diana nursed him back to health. Then, after he had been given a memory-blocking drug to erase his knowledge of the island, she escorted him back to the United States where she adopted the guise of bespectacled Diana Prince and became a secretary in the War Department. By a twirling strip she turned into Wonder Woman, in a red, white and blue costume to signify her commitment to freedom and democracy, fighting Nazi activities with weapons which included bracelets that deflected bullets and a lasso that made captives tell the truth.

In subsequent series the story had leapt on to 1977, Diana had returned to Paradise Island after World War Two but another plane had crashed there, this one flown by Steve Trevor's look-alike son (also played by Lyle Waggoner). Diana went to America again in a re-run, becoming Trevor Junior's assistant in the Inter-Agency Defence Command, fighting mad scientists, aliens and paramilitary organisations.

This series received the backing of women's groups who saw the heroine as a symbol of feminine independence and determination. They liked scenes such as one in which a woman announced, 'I've learned my lesson; I'll rely on myself, not on a man,' and Wonder Woman replied approvingly, 'Don't forget that.' The actress, however, gave them little encouragement. She said: 'My feelings about all that are that I am already liberated and I don't want to be liberated any more. I believe in equal pay and equal opportunity; I believe that the best man or woman should win, but I don't hold with the feeling that the way to achieve this is by hitting someone over the head. I think the way to achieve that is by example and tenacity.'

Space Man, Green Man

Buck Rogers first appeared in American newspapers in 1929 and ran in comic strip form in 450 newspapers around the world until 1967, after which he vanished, but in 1978 it appeared he was not dead. According to *Buck Rogers in the 25th Century* he had been launched on a deep space probe but his rocket had been blown out of its trajectory and he was in deep-frozen hibernation for 500 years, returning to earth in the 25th century. When he awakened from his long sleep he was aboard the flagship of the Draconian fleet, on his way to a peace conference on Earth.

While Rogers had been whizzing out of control in space a nuclear holocaust had wiped out most of civilisation. Life had become concentrated in one enormous computer-governed city in the American midwest. Outside it was Anarchia, a desolate no-man's land populated by criminals and mutants, from where could be seen the rubble of Chicago.

Gil Gerard turned down the first offer to play Rogers: 'I didn't even read the script. All I could envisage was *Wham! Pow!* like Batman, but they came back to me again and pointed out that Buck was different. He was a character with warmth, vulnerability, a sense of humour. There was a humanity and nobility in him. He wasn't a super-human. He was just a man doing heroic things.'

The series brought back all the familiar Rogers characters seen in a 1950 series (with a different cast). There was blonde, blue-eyed colonel Wilma Deering (Erin Gray), Commander of the Earth's defences. ('Deviate from my orders, Captain, and you'll be blown to a thousand vapours,' she warned Rogers.) There were also Draconian Princess Ardala (Pamela Hensley), dark haired and smouldering in daring, vaguely oriental costumes, and earth scientist Dr Huer (Tim O'Connor). A feature-length episode also brought back Buster Crabbe who played Rogers in the original film in 1939.

The Incredible Hulk, another series from the pages of comic books in 1978, was the story of Dr David Banner, a mild, compassionate scientist who could become a man-beast of superhuman strength. Dr Banner (Bill Bixby) was a fugitive, a man on the run from himself, society and the primitive creature he became when angry and

*Bespangled charmer,
Liberace, laughing all the
way to his bank.*

Below left *The Partridge
Family, with David
Cassidy at the back on
the right.*

Below right *Patrick
McGoohan as* The
Prisoner *in a series which
never failed to surprise
and puzzle.*

Martin Shaw and Lewis Collins as the all-action macho heroes of The Professionals.

The A-Team come under fire, and their leader (George Peppard) seeks the source of it.

frustrated. The Hulk (Lou Ferrigno) was 7 ft tall, with a greenish skin, massive hands and extraordinary strength, though his conversation was restricted to enraged grunts. The explanation was that Banner was accidentally injected with an overdose of gamma rays during an experiment on human strength, resulting in a Jekyll and Hyde split that he could not control. The world thought Banner dead; he was actually searching for the answers and antidote.

In the course of his search he met strange adventures. One of the most curious was when Banner, driving his car on a highway, was harried by a huge and menacing lorry; many viewers spotted that the scene came from Steven Spielberg's 1971 TV movie *Duel* starring Dennis Weaver. A spokesman for the production company was unapologetic. 'It is normal practice to use stock film in TV series,' he said. 'We used film from *Airport* in another episode of *The Hulk*. Most fans don't seem to care.'

The producers said the Hulk was based on the fact that a savage spirit lives within the most civilised people. Bixby said: '*The Incredible Hulk* is not a message show, but we do deal with controversial subjects such as child-beating, teenage alcoholism and even psycho-surgery.'

To turn Ferrigno, a former Mr Universe, 6 ft 5 in tall and 19½ stone in weight, into the Hulk, two hours were spent in make-up. He had to be fitted with a rubber nose and forehead, and white contact lenses over his eyes. A green wig was clapped on his head and his body was sprayed with green paint. Surprisingly, perhaps, Ferrigno got fan mail from women. 'They write and say they're in love with me and they want to marry me,' he said. 'They say they love watching me rip my clothes off and they want me to do the same to them.' Children, however, saw him as a jolly green giant. 'I like the Hulk,' wrote a 12-year-old, 'because he's fun.'

The Incredible Hulk *(Lou Ferrigno) hurls himself through a window.*

16
Action Men

Adventurers and Other Heroes

The first British action hero to achieve international fame was Robin Hood, the outlaw who robbed the rich and gave to the poor, for screening of the 143 episodes of *The Adventures of Robin Hood* began on 450 stations in America within a few days of its British debut in 1955. The stories followed the traditional version of the legend, being set in the Nottingham area in the last years of the 12th century when Richard the Lionheart was away on the Crusades in the Holy Land and his brother Prince John levied penal taxes on the people. Sir Robin of Locksley opposed him and became Robin Hood, an outlaw in Sherwood Forest where he recruited a band of followers dedicated to thwarting the prince and the sheriff.

A new and economical technique in TV film-making enabled the unit to turn out a 26-minute programme every four and a half days. Normally in film-making, studio technicians built huge sets on which cameras were lined up, but art director Peter Proud did away with such sets, and substituted interchangeable stock items of scenery such as a baronial fireplace, staircases, corridors and entrance halls mounted on wheels so that they could be moved swiftly into position. Proud said:

'The massive sets used on the cinema screen are lost on the small intimacy of television, so by using smaller sets we can speed up the whole process. We can now change a whole set in six minutes. Instead of taking the camera to the set we take the set to the camera. We use the same items over and over again, but we arrange them differently. The result is that the viewing audience get an impression of many different corridors, rooms and archways. Actually, they are seeing the same pieces of scenery each time; the secret is that we have arranged them in a different sequence so that they look different.'

Proud applied the same technique to scenes purporting to be outdoors. One prop was a real 20 ft-high hollow tree trunk on a fake mossy bank. Mounted on wheels, it was used again and again. Another enormous tree trunk was fabricated out of wood and plaster and had an overhanging banch. When both trees were wheeled into the right position they gave the impression of a forest glade.

The Adventures of Robin Hood was the first costume series filmed in England, its knights and soldiers kitted out in chain mail, but as it took two men to lift a shirt of genuine chain mail and place it over the wearer's head, the effect on television was achieved by using garments of knotted string sprayed with silver paint. Richard Greene played Robin Hood, and the success of the series made him rich enough to retire to Ireland afterwards and breed horses. Bernadette O'Farrell was his first Maid Marian, Donald Pleasance was Prince John, Alan Wheatley was the sheriff, and Alex Gauge a rotund Friar Tuck.

The signature tune, *Robin Hood*, was

ITV's first hit theme. The stirring one
minute and four seconds was sung by Dick
James, backed by the cheers of his nine-year-
old son Stephen and eleven schoolfriends.
Within weeks there were eight other versions
of the song on record.

Television has since returned to Robin
Hood. *The Legend of Robin Hood* was a
BBC series in 1977 in which Nottingham-
born Martin Potter portrayed him as an
early freedom fighter. *Robin of Sherwood*
was an HTV series in 1984 with Michael
Praed (later replaced by Jason Connery, son
of Sean) which invested the story with magic

*Robin (Richard Greene), Friar Tuck (Alexander
Gauge) and Marian (Patricia Driscoll).*

and mysticism, making Robin the offspring
of a pagan god. Neither outdid the original.

In 1956, alongside the Robin Hood set at
Nettlefold studios, Walton-on-Thames, the
set was built for another costume series, *The
Adventures of Sir Lancelot*, which told of
the court of King Arthur and his Knights of
the Round Table in the 14th century. (Arthur
lived much earlier but, the company argued,
different authors down the ages put him in
different times.)

Richard Kimble (David Janssen) on the run on a highway in The Fugitive.

Arthur was played by Ronald Leigh-Hunt, Sir Lancelot by William Russell, Queen Guinevere by Jane Hylton, and Merlin by Cyril Smith, and art director Proud again made a major contribution. His round table, 14 ft in diameter and built from Swedish timber, was in the style of the alleged original table in the Great Hall at Winchester, but Proud had it made in 24 pieces, like a cake, with 7 ft slices that could be pulled out. To obtain a close-up of one knight as the company dined in their Cornish castle, a camera of the time had to get close. So out came a chunk of table and in tracked the camera.

On the Road in the USA

A series that was as American and contemporary as *Robin Hood* and *Lancelot* were

British and historic, was *Route 66*. This was then America's principal motorway, stretching 2,200 miles across eight states from Chicago in the east to Los Angeles in the west. A symbol of the American dream, it was celebrated in the song with the refrain, *Get your kicks on Route 66*. The series concerned two young men travelling it in a Chevrolet in search of adventure, work and a place to settle. It was filmed on location, using real factories, hotels, farms and homes, in 1960, which was nine years before *Easy Rider*.

The main characters were Todd Stiles (Martin Milner), a rich man's son, and Buzz Murdock (George Maharis), a poor man's, but the two actors did not get along; Maharis quit and was replaced by Glen Corbett as Linc Case. The strength of the series, though, was that each of the 116 episodes had guest stars, among whom were Robert Redford, Martin Balsam, Suzanne Pleshette, Tuesday Weld, Cloris Leachman, Signe Hasso, Jack Warden, Peter Lorre, Lon Chaney Jr, Lee Marvin and Bruce Dern.

The Fugitive covered even more of America. It was television's longest running manhunt, extending from 1963 over four years and 120 episodes, the earliest in black and white and later ones in colour. The story was inspired by *Les Misérables*, Victor Hugo's story of Jean Valjean, a peasant on the run for stealing a loaf of bread, and hunted by an implacable policeman. In the series Dr Richard Kimble (David Janssen) returned to his home in Indiana after a brief absence and saw a one-armed man running from the house. Inside he found his wife, Helen, dead. Police were unable to trace a one-armed man and Kimble was arrested, convicted of murder and sentenced to death. (The story was set in Wisconsin until it was realised that the state no longer had the death penalty; it was then relocated in Indiana.)

On the way to the penitentiary the train was derailed, and Kimble escaped, pursued by Police Lt. Philip Gerard (Barry Morse). Kimble went on the run across America, striving both to evade Gerard, and find the one-armed man. Kimble surfaced in most states of the USA, and also in Canada and Mexico, surviving 30 brawls, eight gunshot wounds, four stabbings, amnesia and pneumonia. He was knocked unconscious ten times, blinded temporarily by an explosion and run down by a car. The series captured the imagination of millions around the world. 'Kimble is innocent' appeared in car windows and chalked on walls. A New York psychologist said:

'Ordinary people were bound to take pity on Kimble, a guy who was even more put upon than they were. Here was a regular guy trapped in a perverse set of circumstances. Lieut. Gerard was clearly an agent of the Establishment, and the idea that one lone man should thwart the Establishment week after week for four long years had a vast therapeutic value. Millions were on the run mentally, with Richard Kimble.'

Everyone knew, or thought they knew, how the story would end. In Britain some declared that they had seen the final episode during a visit to the States (although it had not been made), many claimed to have been told the ending by a friend in America, and others had read it in American magazines. Barry Morse said: 'In order not to get into a discussion about the series I would pretend that I was someone else. Sometimes I was a Swiss physician complete with accent, or I'd pretend to be a British anthropologist.'

Fugitive fans were split into two main camps: those who knew the one-armed man was guilty, and those who believed the killer was Lt. Gerard, pursuing Kimble for fear the truth would come out. Critic Barry Norman voiced a minority view when he wrote in the *Daily Mail*: 'I think Kimble is guilty. I think he's a dirty, wife-slaying rat who deserves to be strung up from the nearest lamp-post.' The fact was that the ending was neither written, nor decided in advance. Even the actors did not know how the story would end. Morse said:

'We used to have all kinds of joke endings planned. Our favourite was that the camera would pan slowly towards the lighted window of a large house, pass right through and into a bedroom. There it would focus on the face of a woman lying in bed next to David Janssen. She would then turn to him and say, "Darling, do you know I've just had the most terrible dream . . ." '

It was just a studio joke. No one would

The Saint (Roger Moore) could be smooth – with women as glamorous as Dawn Addams.

an amusement park and corner him on top of a water tower, but Johnson overpowered Kimble and was in the act of pushing him from a ledge when Gerard arrived. Faced with a dilemma, he decided in favour of Kimble and shot Johnson, who made a dying confession.

The series made Janssen internationally known, though he observed ruefully: 'People forgot I made 40 flop films before becoming an overnight star.' It also made him rich. 'In a way it's frightening to me that there was a time in the nation's consciousness when I was almost an institution,' he said.

One curiosity of the series, pointed out by Morse was that 'if you carefully watch the opening sequence of each episode you'll notice that the train from which Kimble escapes has "Chemin de Fer" on the side. They had unfortunately used a French train in a stock shot!'

Sir Lew's Mid-Atlantic Heroes

In Britain Sir Lew Grade, who had begun to aim series at the American market, scored his first big hit with *The Saint* in 1963. Stories of Simon Templar, 'the Robin Hood of crime', came from books and short stories by Leslie Charteris which began to appear in print in 1928. Charteris wrote of the Saint:

'He is a roaring adventurer who loves a fight . . . a dashing daredevil, imperturbable, debonair, preposterously handsome, a pirate or a philanthropist as the occasion demands. He lives for the pursuit of excitement . . . for the one triumphant moment that is his alone.'

Charteris had written three dozen books, which had been translated into many languages and sold 22 million copies throughout the world. He had also written hundreds of short stories. The Saint had featured in comic strips, on radio and in films since 1938. Nine actors had played the Saint by this time but Roger Moore was the first on television. He was chosen partly because his handsome looks and bantering sense of humour made him a natural for the role, and also because he was known to the American public through *Maverick*. Since then he had maintained a home in Hollywood.

The series involved Templar in every kind of adventure from saving a beautiful woman

have believed that such a wild situation would be used in *Dallas* in 1986.

Janssen, weary of being asked the ending, invented an even more outrageous one for gullible reporters: 'Kimble is cleared of the murder and retires to a desert island to recuperate. At sunset he takes a swim. Just before plunging into the surf he pauses, unscrews his wooden arm and tosses it in the sand.'

Then rumours circulated that the end would not solve anything. Kimble was going to go free but there would still be some doubt, so that a further series could be made. On the night in August 1967 that it ended, in America and Britain, Japan, Canada and Australia, streets and bars were unusually quiet as millions stayed home — except in London; every other ITV region screened it but London was 20 weeks behind with transmissions of the series. For the record, viewers saw Kimble track the one-armed man, Fred Johnson (Bill Raisch), to

The Saint could be tough. Although behind bars he is more than a match for the ungodly.

whose husband planned to murder her, to rescuing the kidnapped daughter of an American senator. Beautiful women abounded. Leading ladies in one series alone included Dawn Addams, Jackie Collins, Barbara Murray, Julie Christie and Samantha Eggar. The stories were set all over the world – in New York, London, Miami, Paris, Rome, Geneva, the Bahamas, Spain and Canada. The Saint's car, a yellow Volvo P1800 two-seater sports model with the number plate ST1 (Simon Templar One) was known everywhere.

There were 114 episodes over six years, the first in black and white. They were ideal for the international market and achieved 400 million viewers in 106 countries. In 1978 *The Return of the Saint* starred Ian Ogilvy in place of Moore, who had become the cinema's James Bond.

The runaway success of *The Saint* encouraged Lew Grade into other similar series about modern adventurers, with American actors in the leading roles to ensure sales. The first of them was *The Baron* in 1966, which was the first drama series to be made in England in colour, though it was to be three years before Britain's main channels were allowed to transmit in colour.

The Baron was based on the character created by John Creasey, prolific author of 450 books, whose other heroes included Commander Gideon (also portrayed in a television series). The Baron's real name was John Mannering, a jet-age, Jensen-driving antique dealer who owned the most exclusive shops of their kind in London, Paris and Washington, and who found adventure everywhere, foiling unscrupulous collectors and international crooks. However, he underwent changes in the translation from printed page to screen in the interests of American sales. The Englishman became a Texan and was played by Steve Forrest (younger brother of Dana Andrews). His assistant, an intelligence agent, was played by Sue Lloyd.

Man in a Suitcase, a year later, featured a

135

modern bounty-hunter named McGill (played by Richard Bradford). McGill's first name was reputedly John, but it was never used. He was a taciturn man with a chip on his shoulder because he had been ignominiously dismissed from an American security job, sacrificed in order to protect a defecting scientist. His only possession was a battered old suitcase. With no job and no qualifications except his wits, brawn and espionage experience, he set himself up as a British-based bounty hunter, willing to risk his life anywhere so long as he was paid.

For *The Persuaders*, in 1971, Sir Lew Grade needed two major stars, one British and one American because the heroes were to be Lord Brett Sinclair, an English playboy peer, and Danny Wilde, a self-made rough-diamond millionaire from New York, two wealthy adventurers fighting corruption all over the world. The proposal had come from producer Robert S. Baker: 'The idea of two tough men with a great sense of humour, operating together, intrigued me. While I was working on *The Saint* the idea began to materialise.'

Roger Moore was an obvious choice for the Englishman. For the American Grade wanted Tony Curtis. He went to the United States to try to persuade him. Curtis recalls: 'I asked him, "Do I call you Sir Lewis or Sir Louie?" He said, "Call me anything you like, so long as you do the series." So I said, "OK pal, you're on." '

The storyline had the pair meeting and getting into a fight, after which a retired judge blackmailed them into helping him fight crime. The formula was again one of international settings (France, Spain and Italy), sleek cars and sleeker women – among them Joan Collins, Imogen Hassal, Jennie Linden, Susan George and Catherine Schell.

A year later *The Adventurer* starred Gene Barry as film star Gene Bradley, making an epic every two years and earning so much money that he was able to stake friends in business ventures, thereby becoming a partner in baseball teams, oil wells and motor racing companies. When problems arose he moved in – frequently in disguise and employing his acting talents. He also carried out espionage missions for an estab-

lishment figure, Mr Parminter (Barry Morse).

Originals

Not all popular television series have followed a familiar formula; some have avoided pigeon-holing. One of the most original was *Kung Fu*, the story of a shaven-headed Shaolin priest wandering the American West in the 1870s, searching for an unknown brother. Kwai Chang Caine (played by David Carradine, son of John), was a half-American, half-Chinese orphan brought up in a temple in China, emerging as a monk trained in kung fu, the parent science of karate and judo, which turns aggressive force against the aggressor. A strange, quiet, gentle man preaching inner peace, he had to leave China after killing a prince. The story, which ran to 72 episodes, flashed between polite temple life in China during his boyhood when he was nicknamed Grasshopper, and his hardships in America where he became a champion of railroad building workers, and was forced to defend himself with kung fu, often seen in slow motion.

Carradine was taught kung fu for the series by David Chow, a rich businessman who learned it as a boy in Shanghai. Inspired by his example in the series, many Americans then enrolled for classes and spent their leisure hours chopping at each other.

Another original series was *The Onedin Line*, which began in 1974, starring Peter Gilmore as Capt. James Onedin, master of the *Charlotte Rhodes*, a 19th-century square-rigged, three-masted, top-sailed schooner. He was a kind of working-class Horatio Hornblower, taking his ship to sea in scenes filmed off Dartmouth, and coping with domestic and business problems at home in Liverpool.

It was, said one critic, 'a soap with salt', which the theme music from Khachaturyan's *Spartacus* helped to popularise in 57 countries. Gilmore, who had earlier appeared as a singer in undistinguished musicals, claimed that while the series was showing he spent half his working life abroad, making appearances and receiving gifts of boats in bottles and handkerchiefs embroidered with reef knots. Much of the rest of his time was spent trying to answer letters asking such questions

Man in a Suitcase *becomes Man in a Packing Case; Richard Bradford springs a surprise.*

as: 'Is May the best month for sailing round the Horn?'

The Fall Guy was unusual in that, while it starred Lee Majors, the former *Six Million Dollar Man*, as Colt Seavers, a stuntman who doubled as a bounty hunter, its real stars were genuine stunt men. More than 30 were employed on the series, which began in 1981, but their leaders were Mickey Gilbert, a former rodeo rough rider who stood in for Majors in a dark wig when required, and Bob Braiver, a former PE teacher. Majors admitted: 'I'd never try some of their stunts. They have turned *The Fall Guy* into what it is. Without them we'd be lost. They're the best in the business.'

As often as not stories were written around stunts devised by the two stunt men, rather than having them follow a script-writer's ideas. For one programme they jumped a car on to a moving railway wagon so that Seavers could escape from Las Vegas when all the roads were blocked by villains after his blood. They fed all the details, including wind speed and the angle of the take-off ramp, into a computer, and it told them the train should be travelling at 25 mph and the car at 40 mph. For another episode they wanted a car to appear to be overturned by a helicopter flying above it and trailing a grappling hook. They solved this by fitting a kind of cannon under the car which fired a charge downwards as the vehicle was travelling over soft ground. 'That car rose up and flipped over real slow. It worked perfectly,' said Braiver. They demolished more than a score of cars in the course of the series.

Mercenaries

The A-Team were soldiers of fortune prepared to take on any mission if the money and the cause were right, and they grinned and chomped cigars while they tossed hand grenades and dynamite, shot, punched and wrecked. Ten years earlier they had been soldiers, but were convicted in a military court for a crime allegedly committed at the chaotic close of the Vietnam war. After escaping from military prison they survived in the underground of Los Angeles.

Col. 'Hannibal' Smith (George Peppard), a former career officer, was their leader; BA (for Bad Attitude) Baracus (played by the oddly styled Mr T) was a street-smart black from a Chicago ghetto, a former staff-sergeant who was a mechanical genius but had a fear of flying; Templeton (The Faceman) Peck (Dirk Benedict) was a handsome scrounger and go-getter; and Howling Mad Murdock (Dwight Schultz) was a shell-shocked pilot. They were sometimes joined by Amy Amanda Allen, known as 'Triple A' (Melinda Culea), a reporter for a Los Angeles newspaper. The favourite character, particularly with children, was Baracus, played by Mr T (born Lawrence Tureaud), 5 ft 11 in tall and weighing nearly 16 stone even without the pounds of jewellery that adorned his fingers, wrists, ears and neck. Once a nightclub bouncer and a bodyguard, he had turned actor as a boxer in the film *Rocky III*.

Because of the young viewers it attracted, the series, which began in 1983, was criticised for showing aggression and warfare, and in Britain was cancelled in the wake of the Hungerford massacre when a gunman ran wild in the town and killed 16 people. An American network executive said defensively: 'We're not looking for Emmy nominations but to get viewers' blood pumping. . . . These are crazy times. The A-Team

are underdogs, outcasts of society at a time when there a lot of depressed people – the unemployed and those who are experiencing a poor quality of life. The show is for them. It's escape.'

Much the same might be said for *The Equalizer* in which Robert McCall, a silver-haired, impeccably dressed, music-loving ex-secret agent, ran a one-man crime-fighting operation from a stylish Manhattan apartment, helping those who had exhausted conventional sources of help – sometimes with a Walther PPK. McCall offered his services through a newspaper small advertisement: 'Got a problem? Odds against you? Call the Equalizer.' It listed a telephone number which he called hourly for messages. He then arranged meetings in a cafe, driving himself in a polished black Jaguar. Typical cases handled by McCall, who was estranged from his wife but close to his music student son, Scott (William Zakhai), involved an attractive divorcee harassed by a psychotic, and a child kidnapped by mistake.

McCall was played by English actor Edward Woodward, whose frightening command of controlled anger had been seen on British television in 1967 when he played *Callan*, a cold-blooded, licensed-to-kill secret agent.

Lawyers

Not all heroes are involved in violence. They can also be professional men – lawyers and doctors – and the most popular television lawyer was the courtroom defence attorney *Perry Mason*, who never lost a case. A murder would be investigated by trilby-hatted Lt. Arthur Tragg (Ray Collins) who, with District Attorney Hamilton Burger (William Talman), would build a watertight case. The suspect then went to Mason (Raymond Burr) who would examine the case with his secretary, Della Street (Barbara Hale) and private detective Paul Drake (William Hopper). The case would always look hopeless for Mason's client but during the trial Mason would crack a witness or Paul Drake would uncover vital evidence.

Burr, who had played a succession of bad types in Hollywood, was originally screen-tested for the role of Burger, but when author Erle Stanley Gardner, Mason's creator, saw Burr on film, he leapt up shouting: 'That's him, that's Perry!' Burr played the role for nine years from 1957 and said: 'I tried to approach that witness stand in a different way in every episode.' He ploughed through innumerable legal works, was awarded an honorary Doctor of Law degree by a law college in Sacramento and made numerous appearances for legal organisations.

In the last episode, *The Case of the Final Fade-out*, in 1966, Mason defended a TV star accused of murdering his producer, and Erle Stanley Gardner played the judge. A revival in 1973, *The New Adventures of Perry Mason*, had Monte Markham as Mason, and a different cast, but in 1987 Burr and Hale were reunited in *Perry Mason Returns*, with Mason as a judge.

Perry Mason may have been the most popular legal series but the most respected was *The Defenders*, which began in 1961 with E. G. Marshall and Robert Reed as a crusading father-and-son legal team, Lawrence and Kenneth Preston. Based on a story by Reginald Rose, who wrote *Twelve Angry Men*, every programme dealt with a different ethnical issue such as euthanasia, abortion, civil disobedience, and blacklists – and the Prestons did not always win. The first programme, *The Quality of Mercy*, asked whether a doctor who killed a mongoloid baby at birth was guilty of murder. Gene Hackman played the baby's father and Jack Klugman the DA. Marshall said later: 'We did 32 hour-long shows every year for five years and people still wonder why I gave it up.'

Doctors

A pair of young doctors made their debuts in America within weeks of each other in 1961. *Doctor Kildare* (Richard Chamberlain) was babyfaced and naive; *Ben Casey* (Vince Edwards) was surly and aggressive, but they were rivals in popularity. In the following five years *Kildare* went ahead, then *Casey*, then *Kildare* again. Women were their biggest fans, Kildare appealing mainly to younger ones, Casey to the more mature.

There were other similarities between the two shows. Both young doctors worked in large hospitals, although Kildare was an

A price on his head in place of hair – David Carradine as monk in Kung Fu.

intern or house officer, Casey a neurosurgeon. Both had elderly mentors, Kildare's the crusty Dr Leonard Gillespie (Raymond Massey), Casey's the wizened Dr David Zorba (Sam Jaffe).

Kildare was based on stories by Max Brand and cinema movies which had begun in 1937, with Kildare played most often by Lew Ayres. Chamberlain said:

'Doing Kildare was hard work and marvellous training, but after five years I thought I'd rather exhausted its possibilities. The image of Dr Kildare is exactly how I was when I began the series. The difficulty was that as I grew up, he didn't, so I couldn't either until the series was over. Kildare was a prig, and it was agony speaking to the Press because I could never speak my mind. I always had to say everything was lovely and beautiful and true. On the other hand, I was getting about 12,000 letters a week, which

Instruments at the ready, Raymond Massey as Dr Gillespie, Richard Chamberlain as Dr Kildare.

broke all studio records and I enjoyed that, because all actors love to be adored – that's why they become actors'.

Edwards, who had already played a frontier doctor in Henry Fonda's *The Deputy* series, was one of 60 actors interviewed for *Ben Casey*. After getting the part he spent his spare time investigating neurosurgery. *Ben Casey* was what has become known as an 'Am I going to die, doc?' show but it raised important issues. One episode had Shelley Winters as an unmarried woman, pregnant after an affair with a doctor, and suffering toxaemia, which could threaten her life and that of the unborn baby. Casey urged an abortion; she refused, and the episode ended with the delivery. Other guest stars included Sammy Davis Jr playing a baseball idol who lost an eye in a playing field accident; Davis had actually lost an eye in a car accident.

Both *Kildare* and *Casey* ended in 1966 but Chamberlain and Edwards had made such an impact in their roles that despite all their subsequent success they are still commonly identified in the Press as 'the former Dr Kildare' and 'the former Ben Casey'.

Many medical series followed but none achieved as much success until 1969 when *Marcus Welby MD* presented the story of a family doctor, a general practitioner in a world of specialisation. It reversed the Kildare/Casey formula in that the hero was an elderly man with a young assistant. Welby (played by Robert Young, the Hollywood leading man of the Thirties) was a patient, dedicated, silver-haired widower, practising from his home in Santa Monica, California. Having suffered a heart attack, he had been forced to hire a young associate, Dr Steven Kiley, opinionated and outspoken, making calls on a motorcycle and yearning to be a neurologist. James Brolin, as Kiley, had much the same sort of impact as Chamberlain and Edwards years earlier.

The two doctors were of different generations but they learned from each other. They never seemed to present bills. *Welby* was a series which was all sweetness and light. There are worse formulas for creating an international television hit.

140

INDEX